# STRATEGIES FOR
# THE DISPLACED WORKER

# Strategies for the Displaced Worker

## Confronting Economic Change

George P. Shultz and Arnold R. Weber

Foreword by Clark Kerr

Harper & Row, Publishers, New York and London

LIBRARY OF CONGRESS CATALOG CARD NUMBER: 66-13925
C-Q

# CONTENTS

# Foreword by Clark Kerr

*President, The University of California*

The Automation Fund Committee is a unique private effort, established in collective bargaining, to meet the problems of displacement caused by improved technology. From its establishment in 1959, widespread interest has been shown in the committee's operations. From time to time the committee has released reports on particular aspects of its activities, but now the co-chairman of the committee and one of its staff members have written an analytical history of its experiences which will be of the greatest interest as a benchmark in the new field of labor market adjustment. The authors could be expected to be skilled in economic analysis and research. But beyond that, the report reflects the qualities of imagination and flair which they applied to the problems of finding new jobs for displaced workers. It is also a rare pleasure to encounter a lucid and sometimes vivid style.

When Armour and Company announced in the early summer of 1959 the permanent closing of six major plants, there had already been nine shutdowns in a program of modernization which involved the closing over a fifteen-year period of a total of twenty plants with 13,000 employees. The plan called for the establishment of new plants in other areas, but with many fewer workers because of the dramatic technological improvements in the industry. The 1959 negotiations between Armour and the two unions which had organized its plants, the Amalgamated Meat Cutters and Butcher Workmen and the United Packinghouse, Food and Allied Workers, resulted in the setting up of a tripartite Automation Fund Committee with broad powers to study the problems of displacement resulting from the modernization program, to promote transfers within the company by providing retraining and relocation allowances and to consider other employment opportunities. The pioneering and unconventional action taken by the company and the unions has had constructive results, and one can only express surprise and gratification at how much a relatively modest sum —compared with the substantially larger amounts available to the public agencies in the field—can still accomplish in the right hands. Another unexpected note, as the report observes, is that this dramatic exercise in joint action involved a company and two unions whose relations, far from being unusually harmonious, have in fact been fairly stormy.

For the committee and staff, this experience has been a successful learning process. Over time, an increasing proportion of the workers displaced by plant shutdown have come within the scope of the programs, established alone or in conjunction with government agencies, and progress can be reported in every phase of activity: interplant transfer, placement, retraining. On the other hand, the report makes clear that there is here no panacea, nor any justification for complacency, because the displaced workers are now less well off than they were before.

The final conclusion is that any remedial program must consist of a package of measures, so that workers with marketable skills can be helped immediately by a good placement program; others can benefit from retraining; the transfer option is available for those who want it; and older workers can take advantage of early retirement benefits. The problem for the future is not to devise "bold new ideas," or to call for large expenditures; the committee has found that big programs are fully effective only when they are translated into terms that apply to particular situations, and that retain the flexibility to deal with the individual's problems. This is the essential justification for private efforts, supplementing the great resources of government but no less essential in their emphasis on the individual and on individual needs in reducing the massive effort to the human scale.

I have had the privilege of serving as impartial chairman of the Armour Automation Fund since its inception. George P. Shultz, dean of the Graduate School of Business of the University of Chicago, joined me as co-chairman in 1961, following the resignation as executive director of the committee of Robben W. Fleming, then professor of law at the University of Illinois and now provost at the University of Wisconsin.

The practical worth of the committee hinged to a large degree on the company and union representatives: from the company —Harold E. Brooks, vice president; Walter E. Clark, vice president, Industrial Relations; Clifton B. Cox, vice president, Foods Division; Frederick R. Livingston (Kaye, Scholer, Fierman, Hays and Handler); from Amalgamated Meat Cutters and Butcher Workmen of North America, AFL-CIO—Russell E. Dresser, vice president and director, Packinghouse Division; James H. Wishart, research director; from United Packinghouse Food and Allied Workers, AFL-CIO—Ralph Helstein, president; Jesse Prosten, director of Contract Administration. Experts in their own right, they were both cooperative with and tolerant of their academic colleagues. It has been a personal pleasure to serve with them.

# Preface

This book constitutes an interim report on a continuing experiment in American industrial relations. The focus of the experiment has been a comprehensive effort to cope with mass layoffs within the framework of a collective bargaining relationship. Although the experiences reported here reflect the special circumstances of economic change and union-management relations in one large company, they can provide guides for other parties who are confronted with similar challenges. At the least, they call into question the assumptions that have conditioned the programs for dealing with displaced workers in the past and point out the pitfalls that are likely to be present in the future.

In 1959, Armour and Company and the United Packinghouse and Allied Workers of America and the Amalgamated Meat Cutters and Butcher Workmen of North America established the Automation Fund Committee in response to the labor displacement arising from the modernization program initiated by the company. The committee is organized on a tripartite basis with representatives from the unions, management and the "public." The "public" members have been drawn by the Parties from the ranks of the academic community, reflecting their belief that, although professors have never met a payroll, they may play a useful part when the payroll is stopped. For much of the committee's existence the authors have been such professorial "public" members and have welcomed the opportunity to participate in a venture that has subjected general notions of labor market policy to harsh, pragmatic tests.

The Automation Fund Committee commenced its activities with a broad and imprecise mandate to develop programs that would minimize the impact of economic change on the work force. As these programs have evolved, two unique characteristics

xi

have been identified. First, they have combined efforts to reassign displaced workers within the company with other measures to facilitate the search for new employment in the labor market at large. And second, the committee has developed a pattern of private-public cooperation in the administration of programs for handling labor displacement.

On the first count—the development of programs that span the gap between the firm and the labor market—the committee implemented a complex system for the interplant transfer of displaced employees within Armour and Company and further initiated a program for the retraining and placement of those workers who moved into the labor market beyond the boundaries of the firm. The elaboration of these programs often involved a chain of reactions that the parties could not foresee at their inception.

One example will suffice to illustrate the progressive experimentation that marked the committee's activities. When the Oklahoma City plant closed down in 1960, the committee established a program for the partial financial support of those workers who were interested in retraining for new occupations. The results of this modest effort clearly indicated that retraining would have to be carried out on a broader basis and with more generous financing if it was to be successful. Thus the committee expanded its support of the next retraining venture launched after the shutdown of the Armour plant in Fort Worth, Texas. The results of the Fort Worth project were sufficiently promising so that a similar program was undertaken when another unit was closed in Sioux City, Iowa. However, whereas the training facilities in Fort Worth were generally adequate, Sioux City lacked sufficient educational resources to sustain an effective program. Consequently, several retrainees were sent to schools away from home to receive useful instruction. Once this step was taken, the committee responded to the necessity of providing these trainees with subsistence allowances while they were out of town. At the same time, the initiation of more ambitious training programs meant that the participants were under greater financial pressures which might prevent them from completing their courses. To relieve these pressures, the committee then established a special loan fund for the trainees.

A parallel sequence of reactions could be described for the development of the interplant transfer system.

Clearly, a major strength of collective bargaining in handling large-scale labor displacement is its capacity for continuous innovation in the light of the circumstances of each case. As a result of this process, the committee was able to design sets of options related to the preferences and prospects of the individual worker. In addition, the collective bargaining relationship provided an essential vehicle for the implementation of the programs once they were set in motion. A fundamental lesson of the committee's experiences is that the most artfully conceived plan only has significance to the displaced workers when the parties are committed to the intensive administration of the program over a prolonged period of time. And because the unions and the company have an intimate knowledge of the situation, they can deal effectively with the unique cases and the hard questions of equity that arise when abstract rights are translated into specific actions. A commitment to administration is no guarantee of the success of a program; but without it any effort to help displaced workers is destined to fail.

The same flexibility has characterized the use of government resources by the committee. When the committee undertook its first project in Oklahoma City, public programs for the aid of displaced workers were in their formative stages. Public and private officials had little experience in the area and were seeking to develop adequate mechanisms for handling large-scale displacement and a framework for constructive collaboration. Dissatisfaction with the routine operations of the government agencies, particularly the employment service, persuaded the committee substantially to "go it alone" in its project in Fort Worth. Here, the employment service was used primarily for special technical services such as the testing and preliminary counseling of the displaced workers. However, as the federal manpower development and training program took shape and as the employment service sharpened its techniques for dealing with mass layoffs, the committee altered its strategy to make greater use of government resources in placement and retraining.

The shift in policy had the obvious advantages of conserving the committee's funds and moving the displaced Armour workers into on-going programs where these programs were responsive to their needs. This new approach did not mean that the role of the committee was diminished. Rather, the committee now changed its functions to fit the new circumstances. It helped plan specific measures for Armour workers in cooperation with government officials. It publicized the availability of government programs among the displaced employees and represented them in their dealings with various agencies. And the committee could pinpoint the use of its own resources to do things that were difficult for government agencies.

In effect, the government programs became part of the set of options open to the committee and the individual worker. As the committee pursued its activities in different cities, it learned that there are few fixed laws of comparative advantage in the distribution of responsibility in this problem area between public and private agencies. Instead, the optimal division of labor must be carefully determined in each case. Again, this task requires a basic commitment to administration so that the program can be monitored and perhaps modified, at each stage.

Some readers, especially those in the industrial relations fraternity, will be disappointed that this account does not contain a detailed analysis of the internal deliberations of the Automation Fund Committee. In this respect, we have purposefully resisted the temptation to present an "inside story" of the joint committee approach to collective bargaining. As participants in the committee's activities, we found it difficult to maintain the detachment necessary for objective judgments. Moreover, we feel that the most significant lessons to be derived from the Armour experience are those which relate to the problems of aiding displaced workers. Individual joint study committees inevitably will come and go, but the problems of mitigating the impact of economic change will be a continuing concern in modern industrial society.

Our circumspection should not suggest that the committee's work has been marked with such controversy that, like accounts of political intrigue, it may not be revealed until considerable time has elapsed. To be sure, many of the issues treated by the committee have been contentious as might be expected in a labor-management relationship undergoing a drastic change in its immediate environment. But one of the remarkable aspects of the committee's development has been the extent to which the parties have been able to separate areas of real or potential conflict from the constructive efforts to aid the displaced workers.

We have benefited greatly from the efforts of others in both the conduct of the committee's programs and the writing of this book. We thank the members of the Automation Fund Committee for their willingness to experiment with both professors and labor market policies. In addition, there is a roster of distinguished persons who made major contributions to the committee's work: Professor Clark Kerr, president of the University of California, has guided the committee throughout its existence as its chairman; Professor Robben W. Fleming, presently chancellor of the University of Wisconsin, helped to give the committee its early impetus and directions; Professor Edwin Young, now dean at the University of Wisconsin and president-designate of the University of Maine, directed the pioneering Oklahoma City project; Professor Eaton H. Conant of the University of Chicago was co-director of the Sioux City project and carried it to fruition; and Professor James Stern of the University of Wisconsin has supervised the committee's operations in Kansas City, Missouri and Worthington, Minnesota. A final note of thanks must be given to the committee's most successful retrainees, those women who were drawn from the ranks of the displaced workers and who ran the committee's offices with skill and dedication: In Oklahoma City, Margaret Hostler; in Fort Worth, Maxine Johnson; in Sioux City, Gertrude Wolfe; and in Kansas City, Allie Jones.

We wish also to express our thanks to Harry Dreiser, who made helpful editorial suggestions, and to Barbara Otis and Alease Hargis, who have been most helpful in the preparation of the manuscript.

GEORGE P. SHULTZ
ARNOLD R. WEBER

Chicago, Illinois
November 1, 1965

# STRATEGIES FOR
# THE DISPLACED WORKER

# 1 The Challenge of Labor Displacement

ECONOMIC change has long been an accepted feature of the American scene. As part of the process of adjustment to market forces, manpower and capital have been continually redeployed throughout the economy. The visible evidence of this process is often the shutdown of old, inefficient units of production and the establishment of modern facilities in new locations. In many cases, these shifts in the geographical distribution of industrial activity have given rise to major labor dislocations and severe economic losses to the communities from which the plants have been withdrawn.

It would be difficult to say with any certainty whether or not the tempo of economic change has accelerated in recent years. To be sure, the current concern over "automation" has heightened the public's sensitivity to what were formerly arcane economic events. A broader historical perspective cannot ignore, however, the massive movement of resources that took place in earlier stages of national development. On the other hand, it is clear that attitudes toward the *consequences* of economic change have undergone a significant transformation. In the past, amelioration of the effects of large-scale labor displacement was generally left to the autonomous mechanisms of the labor market. Similarly, communities faced with the problems of plant withdrawal could call upon few resources other than the dwindling stock of optimism of the local Chamber of Commerce.

In recent years, this passive attitude toward economic dislocations has been supplanted in many quarters by a belief that active policies are required to ease the transition to the new set of circumstances of the worker and the community alike. Organized efforts have been launched by state and local authorities to aid displaced workers and distressed areas. These programs have

1

been buttressed by expanded activity and expenditures on the part of the federal government. At the same time unions and managements, acting as private parties, have given increased attention to the fate of their members and employees who must bear the immediate burdens of economic change. To a large degree, such union-management programs have followed the traditional paths worn by decades of collective bargaining. However, the willingness of the parties to expand their activities so as to encompass the fate of the worker in the labor market at large has given a new dimension to industrial relations practice.

This volume reports on the concerted efforts of private parties to deal with the consequences of labor displacement stemming from extensive economic adjustment within a major American corporation. In the mid-1950s Armour and Company, the nation's second largest meat packer, embarked on a program of rationalization that involved the closing of a considerable number of existing plants and the construction of new units removed from the traditional centers of production. When the scope of the reorganization became evident, a series of special measures was taken to cushion its impact on the work force. The starting point of these efforts was the formation of the Automation Fund Committee in 1959 by agreement between the company and the two unions that represented the majority of the affected workers; the Amalgamated Meat Cutters and Butcher Workmen of North America and the United Packinghouse, Food and Allied Workers. The committee is tripartite, including management, union, and public members. It was given a broad mandate to attack the problems of displacement and transition that confronted the parties. This mandate afforded the committee a rare opportunity to initiate action and to evaluate its effects upon the employability and employment experience of displaced workers in a variety of localities and situations.

In many ways, the Armour situation exemplifies the challenges and difficulties of mounting an effective policy of labor market adjustment in the United States today. The characteristics of the workers and the labor markets involved gave little assurance that the problems of adjustment would be resolved either by statements of good intentions or by automatic economic processes. In addition, although the committee's activities were privately initiated and administered, intensive efforts were made to develop close cooperation with various public programs in the same substantive area.

This account of the Armour experience is not calculated to provide an exact blueprint for those who must deal with similar situations. Indeed, one of the lessons to be derived from efforts of the Automation Committee is that a diligent regard for the unique qualities of each case is essential for a modicum of success in handling the problems of labor displacement. Nonetheless, these episodes can have a wider significance by helping to identify certain obvious pitfalls in the administration of a program for the adjustment of displaced workers and by making explicit the various courses of action available to union and management practitioners in the field. Beyond these operational considerations, the Armour experience raises broader questions for the future course of public policies that deal with the same set of economic and human problems.

## Origins of the Committee

Armour and Company is the second largest meatpacker in the United States, with total sales in 1964 of almost $2 billion. In its meatpacking operations the company runs forty-six plants and now employs about 14,500 production workers in all sections of the country. Armour's operations also extend to a variety of other industries, including soap, pharmaceuticals, and chemicals.

The Amalgamated Meat Cutters and Butcher Workmen of North America and the United Packinghouse, Food and Allied Workers, both affiliated with the AFL–CIO, are the dominant unions in the meatpacking industry and each has, in addition, significant membership in other areas. The Amalgamated has long had a large membership among butchers in retailing establishments, and the UPWA has extended its organizational base to other food-processing sectors such as canning and sugar beet processing. The Amalgamated is considerably the older and larger of the two, while the UPWA has more members working in Armour plants.

Relations among the parties frequently have been highly contentious. At the time of the great organizing drives in the late 1930s the Packinghouse Workers Organizing Committee (later UPWA) selected Armour as the leading target for unionization. Consequently, much of the conflict associated with establishing a new basis for labor-management relations in the meatpacking industry was focused on that company. Because Armour has subsequently been a pattern-setter for collective bargaining, continued pressures have been put on the union-management relationship. For several years, these pressures were augmented by the active rivalry between the UPWA and the Amalgamated.[1]

Gradually, however, collective bargaining between Armour and the two meatpacking unions has become more stable. In 1941 the company entered into a master agreement covering all plants organized by the UPWA. A similar contractual arrangement was eventually evolved for the units represented by the Amalgamated, and in 1956 the two unions agreed for the first time to hold joint negotiations with the company.

Within this framework, the Automation Fund Committee was established as a result of the 1959 negotiations. The committee's work has been extended by contracts renegotiated in 1961 and 1964. Despite these general movements toward stable relations, explosive points of contention have remained and these have had

---

[1] For more information on labor-management relations in the industry, see Joel Seidman, "Unity in Meat Packing: Problems and Prospects," in Davey, Kaltenborn, and Ruttenberg (eds.), *New Dimensions in Collective Bargaining* (New York: Harper & Bros., 1959), and Walter Galenson, *The CIO Challenge to the AFL, A History of the American Labor Movement 1935–1941* (Cambridge: Harvard University Press, 1960), esp. Ch. 10: "The Meat Industry," pp. 348–378.

a continuing impact on the committee's work.

Excerpts from the 1959 contract clause establishing the committee suggest the nature of its functions:

The committee is authorized to utilize the fund for the purpose of studying the problems resulting from the modernization program and making recommendations for their solution, promoting employment opportunities within the company for those employees affected, training qualified employees in the knowledge and skill required to perform new and changed jobs so that present employees may be utilized for this purpose to the greatest extent possible, and providing allowances towards moving expenses for employees who transfer from one plant to another of the company's plants. . . .

The committee should also continue to consider other programs and methods that might be employed to promote continued employment opportunities for those affected.

Except as explicitly provided otherwise below, the findings and recommendations of the committee shall not be binding upon the parties, but shall be made to the company and to the unions for their further consideration.[2]

Thus the committee's duties were broadly defined and experimental in nature. Its initial mandate called for intensive study of the problems of displacement and an open-ended consideration of programs that might promote stability of employment. The only specific committee functions related to the administration of initially undefined training and interplant transfer programs and to the determination of "replacement plants" for closed facilities.

The committee's activities were supported by a $500,000 fund created under the terms of the 1959 agreement and financed by contributions from the company. This sum has been more than adequate for the financial support of the programs undertaken by the committee during the first five years of its existence. Initially, most of the funds were expended to finance special research projects that were considered important in guiding the committee

[2] The full text of the clause creating the Automation Fund Committee is in Appendix A.

in the establishment of appropriate programs. Later, the bulk of the funds was allocated to the support of actual projects initiated following the shutdown of specific plants. As subsequently indicated, the funds were used to support a variety of activities, from the payment of retraining expenses to a special loan program for the retrainees. Over-all, the various programs did not put an excessive strain on the available resources; in mid-1965 approximately $140,000 remained of the original $500,000 fund.

## The Magnitude of Displacement

When the Automation Fund Committee was established,[3] the process of rationalization was already well under way within Armour and Company. Between 1951 and 1959 nine small plants had been closed in different parts of the country. The impact of these adjustments had barely diminished when, in the summer of 1959, management announced the permanent shutdown of six major plants, resulting in the displacement of 6,000 workers. Among these units was the main Armour plant in Chicago, which in the past had stimulated poets and union organizers alike to extraordinary efforts.

The formation of the Automation Fund Committee presaged the complete or partial shutdown of five other plants, adding about 5,000 more people to the list of displaced workers. These plants were located in Oklahoma City, Oklahoma; Birmingham, Alabama; Fort Worth, Texas; Sioux City, Iowa; Kansas City, Missouri; and Cleveland, Ohio. They ranged in size from 180 employees in Birmingham to over 1,600 workers in Kansas City. In the fifteen years ending in mid-1965, twenty-one Armour plants employing about 14,000 workers had borne witness to the pervasive reorganization of the meatpacking industry.

During the same period, eight new Armour plants were built. For the greater part, these new units were placed in operation in

[3] For a complete listing of persons who have served in an official or consultative capacity with the committee, see Appendix B.

1963 and 1964. Employment in the new facilities is substantially below the level that prevailed in the old plants. The differences in employment reflect a change in operating methods: in place of the comprehensive, integrated plants engaged in producing a full line of meat products were units specializing in a particular animal and breaking down the slaughtering, butchering, and processing into separate operations. In addition, new technology has permitted sharply increased rates of output per man hour. Thus the aggregate manpower requirements of the eight new plants totaled an estimated 900 workers.

These plant closings, the development of the transfer opportunities to the new units, and efforts to retrain and place the workers in jobs outside the meatpacking industry, were the major objects of the committee's attention in the last five years. It was clear that the committee had to respond immediately to problems of major proportions and could not enjoy the luxury of detailed preparations for a distant challenge.

The displaced Armour workers had dim employment prospects in anything but a tight labor market. For the greater part, skills involved in meatpacking jobs are not transferable to other industries; nor do these jobs call for long periods of education and training. Only about 10 per cent of the typical work force in a large meatpacking plant possess identifiable skills which can be utilized in other industrial situations without supplementary training, and these skills are largely associated with maintenance.

The problem of re-employment was further magnified by the age distribution of the displaced workers. In most of the obsolete plants the median age of the work force ranged from 45 to 48. In Fort Worth, for example, only eight of the 1,000 displaced employees were under 30 years of age. Many of these workers had been hired during the labor shortage of World War II and shortly thereafter; they had accumulated an average of twenty years' seniority. This extended attachment to industry and company implied that most of the workers had been removed from job-seeking activity in the labor market for a long time.

The educational level of the work force also did not facilitate the task of re-employment. In most of the closed plants, the median did not exceed eight grades of formal schooling. In addition, the displaced workers generally had been away from any formal educational situation for many years.

The sex composition of the displaced workers was predominantly male; the proportion of females ranged from 12 to 15 per cent. The women generally had a higher average age than the men, thus presenting special problems of transition and adjustment.

The relative importance of minority groups in the work force varied considerably among the five plants. In Sioux City about 5 per cent of the workers were either Negroes or American Indians, whereas Negroes comprised approximately 75 per cent of the plant labor force in Kansas City. Fort Worth, Texas represented an intermediate case, with 35 per cent Negro and 15 per cent Latin American employees. At the time of the shutdown, the school system in Fort Worth was completely segregated on a white-Negro basis and definite patterns of job discrimination applied to Negroes and Latin Americans alike.

As a whole, the displaced workers were characterized by low education, high age, long attachment to a particular industry and plant, and special disabilities connected with ethnic or racial identifications. By the usual standards, this group faced special problems in making the transition to new employment, and these problems were not offset by conditions in the local labor markets. To be sure, these markets are urban, and typically have a large and diverse array of jobs. In all cases but one, however, the local unemployment rate exceeded 5 per cent at the time of the shutdown, or worsened considerably during the period when displaced persons were seeking employment. Sioux City enjoyed a relatively low unemployment rate at the time of the shutdown, but the relatively small size of the labor market and the limited number of jobs in manufacturing made absorption of a large number of workers difficult.

The reductions in employment in Armour and Company were

sharp and precipitous, rather than gradual. This meant that a large number of workers with similar characteristics were seeking work at the same time. More significantly, however, the abruptness of the action ruled out the use of the traditional and limited remedies to ease the impact of change, such as attrition or early retirement. Similarly, expanded bumping rights within the plant for senior employees could not be exercised; any effort to avert the displacement of older, high-seniority employees, if it could be made at all, would have to be made within corporation-wide units of economic opportunity. An alternative approach strongly indicated by the circumstances was to increase the employability of the displaced workers through intensive efforts at retraining and by a vigorous campaign to identify new job opportunities.

## The Nature and Evolution of the Committee's Functions

The unfolding of these problems determined the agenda of the committee's activities. In approaching its tasks, the committee and the parties moved from an initial stage of fact-finding and experiment to the modification of existing policies through revision of the labor agreement, and then to a period of intensive administrative effort. This evolution of tasks and emphases was not "planned" in the sense that the parties laid out a neat progressive sequence of activities. Instead, the different stages of development reflected a series of short-run, pragmatic responses by the committee to the problems posed by major events in the union-management relationship. Nonetheless, each stage clearly laid the groundwork for the next phase so that in retrospect the committee's efforts did have an over-all logic.

The first stage—that of fact-finding and experiment—began with comprehensive studies to assess the dimensions of the problem and to investigate the devices used in other situations to minimize the consequences of large-scale displacement.[4] Postshutdown surveys of the subsequent labor market experience of

[4] For a list of publicly available materials reflecting work done by or for the committee, see Appendix C.

the displaced Armour workers revealed that many of the former employees had encountered great difficulties in finding any work at all, let alone any with adequate wages and satisfactory working conditions. Two years after the shutdown, a careful study in five cities showed that the unemployment rates of the displaced meat-packing workers remained at a distressingly high level, ranging from 25 per cent to 53 per cent. The incidence of unemployment was particularly high for older workers, members of minority groups, the unskilled, and the unschooled.

Another study explored the long-run prospects for employment throughout the meatpacking industry, with results that were not particularly conclusive from the committee's standpoint. At the same time, two additional research projects commissioned by the committee were to examine the policies adopted in other industries regarding the advance notice of plant shutdown and the interplant transfer of displaced workers.

While the parties were engaged in this fact-finding stage, the Armour plant at Oklahoma City was closed, displacing over 400 workers. This event provided the stimulus for the first remedial program initiated by the Automation Fund Committee. Soon after the shutdown, an experimental effort was launched to aid in the placement and retraining of the displaced workers. The program also involved preliminary measures to implement the concept of interplant transfer. The Oklahoma City shutdown was followed by the advent of other employment opportunities in the company when the first of the new plants was opened in Lubbock, Texas. The plant work force was hired from the local labor market, and a sharp controversy ensued over the question of which, if either, of the two meatpacking unions would represent these workers. Ultimately, the United Packinghouse Workers Union won representation rights through NLRB election procedures; but the controversy was renewed over the applicability of conditions specified in the master agreement to this unit.

These experiences, the insights provided by the special research projects, and the experiments carried out after the Oklahoma City shutdown were all matters to be considered during the renegotiation of the collective agreement in the summer of 1961. Consequently, two existing clauses in the contract were changed to aid those who might be displaced by subsequent shutdowns. The schedule of severance payments was increased; under the new formula, employees displaced at Fort Worth and Sioux City collected lump sum payments that averaged approximately $3,000 per employee. Thus substantial direct costs were imposed on the company in the case of a shutdown that had brought large-scale layoffs. In addition, the retirement plan was changed so that employees with at least twenty years of service who had reached the age of 55 were eligible for special early-retirement benefits in the event of plant shutdown. Similarly, those who satisfied the twenty-year service requirement and who were between 60 and 65 years of age were eligible for improved pension benefits. These improvements in employee benefits carried the tacit assumptions that the program of modernization and plant shutdowns was not at an end, and that it would not be possible to provide jobs for all incumbent workers.

Added to the elaboration of these existing contract clauses were three new concepts, each of which reflected the experiences and research of the committee's first two years. Together, they strengthened the framework within which the problems of displacement could be handled.

First, the company was obliged to give a minimum of 90 days' advance notice of plant shutdowns. During this period all employees on the payroll were guaranteed 40 hours of employment each week. Thus a short period was provided during which the employees could consider various options, and the parties, both individually and through the offices of the Automation Fund Committee, could develop measures tailored to the circumstances and the needs of the employees.

Second, the details of an interplant transfer program were agreed upon in an effort to take advantage of the attrition that might occur in all other existing plants organized by the same union. While it was not possible to provide for the exercise of seniority and "bumping" rights on a company-wide basis, it was agreed that displaced workers should have a preferred claim on any job held by an employee hired after the date of agreement regarding the transfer plan. The financial needs of employees for the period between layoff and transfer, and the costs of relocation, were also given contractual recognition. All employees with five or more years of service could claim Technological Adjustment Pay (TAP) amounting to $65 per week, including unemployment compensation benefits and a relocation allowance up to a maximum of $525.

Third, an important supplementary issue concerning the operation of the transfer plan involved the rights of present workers to jobs in new "replacement plants." Although it was agreed that displaced workers had a preferred claim to jobs in "replacement plants," this concept was not spelled out in detail in the contract. Instead, the issue was left for determination by the Automation Fund Committee on a case-by-case basis.

The establishment of a 90-day notice period and the elaboration of the interplant transfer plan and its supporting system of benefits afforded the employees and the parties greater flexibility in responding to plant shutdowns. In addition, the earlier experience in Oklahoma City made the committee vividly aware of the difficulties of mounting an effective program to deal with large-scale displacement. In the succeeding three years, the committee engaged in concerted administrative efforts to apply its policies and techniques in Fort Worth, Texas; in Sioux City, Iowa; and in Kansas City, Missouri. Each case was different from the others and required continued refinement of approach.

These administrative efforts, it should be noted, took place within the context of a labor-management relationship marked by more than usual acrimony. The readjustment process under way was broad in scope and the stakes for the unions and management, let alone the employees, were high. Accordingly, one of the real tasks of the committee was to separate areas of constructive

collaboration, such as a retraining effort, from matters of controversy, while playing as useful a role as possible in resolving the
points at issue.

The cumulative experience culminated in a fresh appraisal of
the problems and of the policy framework within which they were
being resolved. Additional research was now oriented toward ex-
tracting the relevant lessons from specific committee projects.
Further discussions within the committee have aimed at the development of a more comprehensive plan for handling subsequent
changes in the location, number, and structure of employment
opportunities. These continuing deliberations reflected the obvious fact that the attempted solutions had not yet caught up with
the problems. Yet with the continuation of the committee's existence by agreement in contracts negotiated for a three-year term
starting September 1, 1964, all the parties renewed their commitment to the committee's objectives, notwithstanding earlier frustrations.

## Plan of the Book

Subsequent chapters will examine the experiences of the
Automation Fund Committee with the principal methods it used
to deal with displacement. The discussion will focus on the operation of the interplant transfer plan, consider the effectiveness of
the various "financial cushions" in mitigating the economic consequences of displacement, and then proceed to an examination
of placement campaigns in the labor market and programs for
occupational retraining. Special attention also will be given to
the committee's experiences in working with community groups
and government agencies. A final chapter will attempt to pull
various threads together and will present some views concerning
manpower policy at the corporate and national levels.

Although several situations are noted in the following chapters,
primary attention is given to the committee's activities with respect to the closing of Armour plants in four cities: Oklahoma

City, Oklahoma; Fort Worth, Texas; Sioux City, Iowa; and Kansas City, Missouri. The period covered extends from 1960 to mid-1965.

However, before beginning a specific discussion of the Automation Fund Committee's activities it will be useful to step back for a more general look at the various programs and techniques developed to deal with the problems of displacement by private and public agencies. In this area, the committee both drew upon and contributed to the total body of experience.

# 2

## Variety in Adjustment to Economic Change: The Contribution of Collective Bargaining

IN approaching the problems of large-scale labor displacement the Automation Fund Committee was traversing a well-worn path in American labor-management relations. Historically, job security has ranked with increased wages as a dominant goal of trade unions in collective bargaining. In recent years, employment security has received renewed emphasis as a bargaining issue in the face of dislocations arising from technological and other forms of economic change. The pressures generated by a rapidly changing economy have found expression in a variety of programs intended to cope with actual or impending labor displacement within the framework of collective bargaining.

Unlike many of the tactics adopted by unions in the past, however, few contemporary programs have sought to avert labor displacement by blocking the precipitating set of economic innovations.[1] Similarly, employers have become increasingly conscious of the need to minimize the cost of the changes to its work force. For the greater part, both unions and management have adhered to a broad policy of benign administration in attempting to cope with actual or imminent labor displacement. Under current conditions, this policy has led to a variety of measures to conserve and allocate job opportunities within the firm and to ease the transi-

[1] For a discussion of historical union policies toward technical change, see Sumner Slichter, *Union Policies and Industrial Management* (Washington, D.C.: The Brookings Institution, 1941), Ch. VII–IX.

15

tion to the labor market at large of those who must bear the burden of displacement. Thus, the Automation Fund Committee had a wide range of industrial relations practice on which to draw in the course of its efforts. The fundamental task of the committee has been to formulate programs that exploit the lessons learned elsewhere while permitting adaptation and innovation in the light of the special circumstances of the Armour situation.

As a backdrop to an account of the committee's activities it is therefore useful to present a broad survey of contemporary labor-management programs for handling the effects upon employment of economic change. In addition, brief consideration will be given to government programs that focus on the same problem area. Together, these private and public programs provide a range of complementary resources from which a strategy for adjustment to change may be devised.

## Programs Under Collective Bargaining

The "management of change" through collective bargaining involves a variety of procedural and substantive measures. These measures may be grouped into four broad categories: (1) the use of normal and induced attrition and of advance notice; (2) the sharing of available job opportunities; (3) economic guarantees and indemnification; and (4) facilitating the transition to work in the labor market beyond the firm. Together, the various categories provide a sequence of defenses against the effects upon employment of economic and technological change. Where one group of measures is inadequate or inappropriate to the task, the parties are likely to fall back to the next line of defense. Success in handling the problems of adjustment may be determined by the selection of that combination of complementary methods that is most suitable to the particular circumstances and traditions of each labor-management relationship.

## 1. ATTRITION AND ADVANCE NOTICE

### Advance Notice

As any banker will assert, time is money and an important element in the operation of the firm. Similarly, time can be vital in dealing with the dislocations arising from change. New methods of operation and production are seldom introduced overnight. Instead, a considerable period of time often is required from inception to implementation. A changeover to dial operations in the telephone industry may take as long as three years. The introduction of computer-controlled production in a steel rolling mill requires painstaking preparation before the first button is pushed. During this period, certain normal administrative and economic processes can reduce the impact of the change on the work force.

First of all, the time lag in the introduction of technical change can be used to provide advance notice to the employees and the union. Within this framework, a comprehensive plan may be formulated to ease the necessary manpower adjustments. Such a plan may not solve the problems of change, but it is the procedural prerequisite for constructive action.

Since the possible benefits of advance notice of large-scale displacement associated with technological change are so obvious, it is surprising to note that they rarely have been incorporated into labor-management agreements in the United States. The typical advance-notice clause requires no more than one week's prior notification of layoff and applies to all cases of retrenchment, without any attempt to vary the period of notice with respect to the cause of the displacement. Originally, many of these traditional clauses served to relieve the employer of any obligation to provide displaced workers with dismissal compensation. As such, they are designed to handle marginal fluctuations in the size of the work force rather than the drastic adjustments occasioned by technical change and/or plant shutdowns.[2]

[2] For a discussion of the functions of layoff notice and an analysis of contract provisions dealing with advance notice, see Theodore Rose, "Layoff, Recall,

The apparent reluctance of management to agree to advance-notice provisions tailored to the requirements of mass displacements arises from certain delicate economic and tactical considerations. In some cases, management may feel that advance information will have a harmful effect on the workers' morale and productivity. The employer may also be concerned that the full disclosure necessary for collaborative planning will lead to efforts by the union to block or encumber the use of the new technology: unlike the subject of Aesop's fable, management is not eager to send the fox to guard the chickens. On the other hand, there is the question of whether union leaders can—or should—adopt a "statesmanlike" pose in the face of pressure from their members, for whom the introduction of change may mean chronic unemployment. Beyond these considerations of strategy, the objection is raised that a fixed-term period of advance notice, involving an implicit guarantee of employment during this period, is not feasible because the time required to introduce the new technology or to shut down an old facility will vary widely from case to case. Thus the maximum period of notice must be limited to the actual period permitted by the character of the new technology and the operational requirements of the firm, or excessive costs will be imposed upon management.

Although these problems are real enough, available evidence indicates that they are generally exaggerated and that the benefits of advance notice will exceed the possible costs. A study of thirty-two cases involving extended advance notice of displacement revealed that once the initial shock of the announcement passed, productivity typically was maintained at previous levels, especially where the notice was linked to the development of a

---

and Work-Sharing Procedures: II. Union Participation in Layoff Procedures; Advance Notice of Layoffs," *Monthly Labor Review* (January, 1957), pp. 1–7. For a discussion of advance notice in the particular context of plant shutdowns see also Arnold R. Weber and David P. Taylor, "Procedures for Employee Displacement: Advance Notice of Plant Shutdown," *Journal of Business* (July, 1963), pp. 302–315.

remedial program. Indeed, in some cases productivity actually increased as workers under incentive pay systems sought to accumulate the largest possible earnings before the shutdown actually occurred. A related fear, that "key" employees would leave the firm in search of other jobs once the impending shutdown was announced, also proved to be overstated. In most of the cases studied, some kind of severance pay arrangement was in effect and since the "key" employees were usually the most senior, the promise of a substantial termination allowance had a marked holding effect upon them.[3]

In recent years, a reconsideration of the problems of advance notice and a concern for public relations have caused many firms to relax their opposition to such clauses. Moreover, unions increasingly have adopted the position that any costs arising from the administration of advance-notice provisions must be accepted by management along with other costs of introducing technological change. Thus, the period of advance notice becomes negotiable in the same sense as other economic matters.

These shifts in attitude and assumptions have paved the way for the negotiation of advance-notice clauses in a growing number of contracts. Ninety-day advance-notice clauses are standard provisions in the "automation agreements" negotiated by the Brotherhood of Railway Clerks and various carriers to handle the introduction of electronic data-processing systems.[4] A few comparable clauses also are found in the chemical and petroleum refining industries.[5] It is also significant that one of the first contractual changes encouraged by the Automation Fund Committee was the provision requiring a 90 days' advance notice of the shutdown of a plant or a major department. The parties agreed that some prior notification was necessary to plan an effective

---

[3] Weber and Taylor, *ibid.*
[4] Cf. agreement between the Brotherhood of Railway Clerks and the Chicago, Milwaukee, St. Paul and Pacific Railroad.
[5] Max D. Kossoris, *Methods of Adjusting to Automation and Technological Change, A Review of Selected Methods Prepared for the President's Committee on Labor-Management Policy* (U.S. Department of Labor, 1964), p. 2.

program for dealing with large-scale displacement.

As in other areas of collective bargaining, the absence of a specific contract clause does not preclude an accommodation on the advance-notice issue. Thus, many employers have provided extended notice of large-scale displacement without any contractual obligation but within the framework of a bargaining relationship. One large chemical producer gave twenty-eight months' notice of a major technical change, and International Harvester notified the United Auto Workers Union of the scheduled shutdown of its McCormick Works three years before the event. In the Bell Telephone System, management has consistently given three years' notice of a conversion to the dial system.[6] Many examples of extracontractual advance notice have arisen in union-management situations characterized by an elaborate system of fringe benefits and seniority rights. Apparently, the existence of complex substantive provisions determining the alternatives available to displaced workers has induced management to modify its notification procedures in order to administer properly the relevant sections of the contract.

### The Joint Study Committee

Another widely heralded innovation in collective bargaining procedures—the joint study committee—also has provided an informal channel for advance notice of technological change. Usually, these study committees have not been formed to deal explicitly with the problems arising from new technology. However, when a firm is entering into a period of substantial technical and economic change, programs to cope with the resultant dislocations are likely to dominate the joint discussions. The Kaiser Long Range Committee has devoted much of its attention to

[6] Harold H. Schroeder, "Employee and Community Relations Problems Resulting from Technological Development," *Michigan Business Review* (July, 1957). Officials of some companies in the Bell System report that as much as five years' advance notice has been given in a few cases.

assessing the probable consequences of new methods of production and to developing a formula for distributing the gains from technical progress. In a broader framework, thirty-four representatives of the newspaper industry and the unions with representation in that industry met to consider measures for dealing with problems arising from accelerating technical change and from adjustments in the organization of the industry.[7] It is not a coincidence that the study-committee approach has been most widely adopted in those industries in which the pace and nature of economic change have posed severe threats to the stability of union-management relations. In this manner, a new collective bargaining institution has emerged on the scene to promote prior notification and planning, even though the discussions may not be characterized in these terms.

The Automation Fund Committee clearly falls within the broad category of the joint study committee. As such, it constituted one response to the impact of the severe adjustments at Armour and Company in labor-management relations. Moreover, the committee has been an important forum for considering the implications of the company's modernization program within a framework that extends beyond the requirements of the 90-day notification clause.

## The Attrition Approach

Once a procedure for advance notice and planning has been established, other normal economic processes can be employed to mitigate the effects of changing technology upon employment. Just as technical change is a fact of economic life, labor turnover may also be expected to occur in each firm and industry. As a recognition of this, the "attrition" approach is a widely endorsed method for handling some of the dislocations associated with technical change. Indeed, a familiarity with this approach can be

[7] *Wall Street Journal*, January 20, 1964.

used as a literacy test among personnel managers and union representatives today.

Notwithstanding the general acceptance of attrition as a basic remedy for the problems of displacement, there are hard problems in making it an effective instrument of manpower policy. The attrition approach works best when the rate of contraction of the labor force owing to resignations, deaths, and retirement is approximately equal to or greater than the rate of displacement generated by the technological change. Where this condition prevails, the "natural" attrition rate can be used to administer an orderly reduction of employment opportunities while minimizing net displacement. If turnover exceeds the immediate displacement, short-term labor requirements can be met by hiring temporary employees or by offering overtime to members of the incumbent work force.

In the Kaiser Steel case, the elaborate program for easing adjustments to technical change was based on the expectation, derived from prior experience, that both the natural attrition rate and the decline in employment opportunities induced by new methods of production would be approximately 8 per cent per year.[8] On the New York City subway system, total employment was reduced by 7,500 workers over a five-year period entirely through reliance on natural attrition. In 1962 this practice was given contractual status in the agreement between the New York Transit Authority and the Transport Workers Union.[9] In the telephone industry, attrition has been widely used as an all-purpose solution to the problems of technological change.

In other cases, however, the healing powers of "natural" attrition may not be equal to the ills inflicted on the work force by economic change. On the one hand, the rate of attrition in each situation will be influenced by factors such as the sex, age, and

[8] David Cole, "The Kaiser-Steel Workers Long Range Sharing Plan: Has It General Application?" in *Jobs, Men and Machines*, edited by Charles Markham (New York: Praeger, 1963), p. 67.
[9] Kossoris, *op. cit.*, p. 4.

seniority distribution of the employees. Although in the telephone industry these considerations have supported a beneficently high attrition rate, turnover may be minimal in other sectors, such as petroleum refining and chemicals. In addition, the union may be reluctant to trust to "natural" attrition for fear that management will increase "normal" turnover by making working conditions move onerous, and by engaging in other forms of harassment.

Where natural attrition appears unequal to the task, the parties may manipulate either the rate of job abolition or the rate of turnover in order to make the attrition approach a sharper tool for manpower planning. In the railroad industry, the use of natural attrition has been modified to permit "controlled" attrition. Under a system of "controlled" attrition, the rate of decline in the number of positions is subject to explicit limitation by the collective bargaining agreement. In the pioneering agreement between the Southern Pacific Railroad and the Order of Railroad Telegraphers, the number of jobs that could be eliminated by attrition was limited to 2 per cent per year.[10] Although several reasons were offered for the imposition of this ceiling, union spokesmen emphasized their concern that management would increase the turnover by a variety of tactics.[11]

Whereas "controlled" attrition attempts to manipulate the decline in job opportunities, "induced" attrition seeks to balance turnover with the rate of displacement by promoting the withdrawal of employees from the firm or labor market. For the greater part, this strategy has taken the form of providing incentives for early retirement. At first, these inducements were offered only where technological change was manifested in immediate, large-scale displacement involving the shutdown of a plant or a major department. Obviously "natural" attrition alone could not absorb the resultant job losses. One method for easing the blow is

[10] Agreement between the Order of Railroad Telegraphers and the Southern Pacific Railroad, October, 1961.
[11] Jack Frye, "Attrition in Job Elimination," Labor Law Journal (September, 1963), pp. 815–816.

to encourage exit from the labor market. Consequently, generous early-retirement benefits have been offered to displaced employees who qualify—usually those with at least twenty years of service who are at least fifty-five years of age. Such plans have been negotiated in the meatpacking, automobile, steel, and petroleum refining industries, among others.

Currently, efforts have been made to induce attrition through early retirement before the actual occurrence of displacement rather than under the special circumstances of a major dislocation. Thus, many industrial unions are pressing for retirement with full pension benefits at age 62 instead of 65. Significant breakthroughs have been registered on this issue in the rubber and oil refining industries.[12] In addition, the normal retirement age was lowered to 60 in the automobile industry following the 1964 contract negotiations.

The drive for early retirement probably has achieved its most spectacular success in the maritime industry. When the shipping companies served notice of the introduction of "automated" ships, the National Maritime Union was confronted with the prospect of a 25 per cent reduction in crew size. Initially, the NMU staunchly resisted any reduction in manning requirements. Ultimately, however, the union agreed to cuts in crew size on automated ships but exacted a *quid pro quo* in the form of early retirement, permitting any seaman with twenty years of service to retire at full pension, regardless of age.[13] This approach was also accepted by the Marine Engineers Benevolent Association, and subsequently was incorporated in contracts between the MEBA and the steel companies that operate ore-carrying vessels on the Great Lakes.[14]

[12] *Wall Street Journal*, July 13, 1964. The breakthrough on early retirement at age 62 with full benefits was achieved at Goodyear, Firestone, and General Tire in the rubber industry. In oil refining, early retirement was put into effect at Sinclair. Similar programs have been subsequently negotiated in the automobile and steel industries.
[13] *Wall Street Journal*, March 25, 1964.
[14] *Wall Street Journal*, April 10, 1964.

Other inducements to early retirement have taken the form of special bonuses in addition to the regular pensions. In the West Coast longshore case, the International Longshoreman's and Warehouseman's Union and the Pacific Maritime Association sought to introduce an attrition cushion against the anticipated contraction in job opportunities arising from the far-reaching revision of work rules. This was done by offering registered longshoremen who were 62 or older, and who had twenty-five years of service, monthly payments of $220 over a three-year period, for a total of $7,920. This effort to promote attrition succeeded beyond the expectations of the parties. In the period preceding the negotiation of the contract, the "natural" attrition rate was approximately 4 per cent per year; in the succeeding two years, the rate of turnover rose to 6.6 per cent. Between 1961 and October 1, 1963, over 1,600 men out of 13,000 dockworkers covered by the contract availed themselves of the opportunity for early retirement. As a result, additional workers were moved into the class of "registered" longshoremen to fill the current manpower demands.[15]

The programs developed by the Packinghouse Workers, the Amalgamated Meat Cutters, and Armour and Company also have attempted to exploit the latitude afforded by attrition. As will be seen, the interplant transfer program, in large measure, has been a devise for the utilization of natural attrition on a company-wide basis. Similarly, the parties have adopted various forms of "induced attrition" to preserve employment opportunities for younger workers. Initially, special early-retirement benefits were available only to workers who were displaced as a result of a plant shutdown. In 1964, however, the regular pension plan was amended to permit early retirement with standard benefits to any worker who met specified service requirements. Although its efforts have been graced with only limited success, the Automa-

[15] Lincoln Fairley, "The ILWU Mechanization and Modernization Agreement: The Union's Point of View," *Proceedings of the Sixteenth Annual Meeting of the Industrial Relations Research Association*, 1963, pp. 38–39.

tion Fund Committee has attempted to use both natural and induced attrition as primary elements in a comprehensive program for manpower adjustments.

*Conclusions*

Despite the problems of application, the use of various administrative and economic processes can afford the parties considerable latitude in adjusting to innovations, especially when there is ample lead time. Undeniably, any program to deal through collective bargaining with the effects of economic change upon employment must begin with an attempt to exploit the possibilities afforded by the time lag in the introduction of these changes and the turnover of the labor force. Indeed, the adroit use of attrition and advance planning will influence to a substantial degree the feasibility and effectiveness of other techniques for amelioration.

By themselves, attrition and advance notification do not have unlimited curative power. The permissible period of advance notice might not be coextensive with the "long run" that economists have proclaimed as the appropriate period for the felicitous adjustment to technical change. Also, once the short-service employees, who have the highest turnover rates, and the existing older workers are siphoned off from the firm's labor force, a substantial residue of potential unemployment may remain. In that circumstance, unions and management are likely to use stronger medicine.

## II. Sharing Available Job Opportunities

The contraction of employment beyond the capacity for adjustment of normal economic processes inevitably gives rise to pressures for the sharing of available or prospective job opportunities. For American unions the effort to distribute job opportunities among their members has been a traditional response to scarcity in the labor market. The particular method of distribution may vary, however, with the incidence of labor displacement. Where the burden of displacement falls most heavily on a few departments or plants, programs will be sought to expand the unit of employment opportunities. In contrast, when the impact of new technology is evenly felt throughout the work force in a given industry or bargaining unit, the union is likely to strive for a reduction in the hours of work on a daily or annual basis. Because the employment effects of technical and economic change are highly variable, elements of both approaches may be incorporated into any program for sharing available job opportunities. In addition, the employer is not indifferent to the policies espoused by the union, and his preferences may have a decided influence on the approach that is ultimately adopted.

### Expanding the Unit of Employment Opportunity

The unit of economic opportunity may be expanded by modifying the seniority system in the plant, by developing formal channels of access to new occupational categories, or through the establishment of interplant transfer systems. The first step involves the broadening of seniority units in a plant so that senior workers who are confronted with the prospect of displacement can bump junior employees across departmental lines. This step has been taken in an increasing number of situations. For example, the 1964 contract between the United Mine Workers and the bituminous coal operators, establishing mine-wide seniority units as part of a program to deal with technological displacement, represents a dramatic departure from previous practice in the industry.[16]

Nonetheless, the problems of developing broad seniority units that balance considerations of equity and efficiency are formidable. Complicated sequences of bumping, the lags introduced by probationary periods on new jobs, and the wide spread of earnings among the jobs pose problems that strain the legendary wis-

[16] *Wall Street Journal*, March 25, 1964.

dom of the shop steward, if not the patience of the personnel manager. In addition, political tensions within the union are likely to become acute where the modification of seniority units means that one worker may then assert a privileged claim to the job of another worker at a time when aggregate employment opportunities in the plant are contracting.

For these reasons, the expansion of seniority units generally has taken the form of broadening or establishing a labor pool at the bottom of the plant's occupational structure. Under this arrangement, workers who are displaced from a department move into the pool where plant seniority governs the relative position of the various workers. Such an approach has been used with some frequency in the chemical industry and is included in the comprehensive displacement program negotiated by Dow Chemical and District 50 of the UMW.[17] The 1962 agreement in the basic steel industry also created a labor pool at the bottom of the occupational structure.

Although they might avert problems of equity, these innovations suffer from an inherent shortcoming as devices for sharing job opportunities: while they afford the senior worker greater immunity from the consequences of technical change, the brunt of unemployment will necessarily be borne by other, junior workers. In order to overcome this limitation, some unions have sought to expand the unit of economic opportunity to include occupational sectors in which the number of jobs has been relatively stable or increasing. For example, the UAW successfully pressed for removal of age barriers to enrollment in apprenticeship programs for the maintenance trades in the automobile companies. Thus, workers who are vulnerable to technological unemployment can move into an area where the long-run economic climate is more favorable.

Considerable success also has been achieved in developing formal channels of access to new occupational categories in the

[17] *Recent Collective Bargaining and Technological Change*, U.S. Department of Labor, Bureau of Labor Statistics, Report No. 266, March, 1964, p. 3.

airline industry. The introduction of jet aircraft has rapidly undermined the technical position of the flight engineer. A series of government boards have supported the contention that the third man in the flight crew should be a qualified pilot rather than a flight engineer. On several airlines, including TWA, United, and American, the flight engineers have been given the opportunity to qualify as commercial pilots. In addition, the newly versatile engineers may be given preference for pilot positions as these open up.[18] Ironically, this model program for promoting lateral occupational movements has been accepted only grudgingly by the Flight Engineers International Union. Their reluctance is founded on the belief that the plan would deal a heavy and perhaps irremediable blow to the existence of the union itself.

The inadequacies of programs to distribute jobs within single plants have stimulated efforts to broaden the unit of economic opportunity to include entire companies, especially where technical change results in the shutdown of a major department or an entire plant. This option, of course, may be exercised only when multiplant firms are involved and, normally, where one union holds representation rights in a large number of units within the particular corporation. The transfer system may apply both to new plants and to established facilities. These plans have been developed in the automobile, can, glass, agricultural implement, railroad, and soap industries. Recently, they have been extended to meatpacking and basic steel.

The decision to establish an interplant transfer system is merely the beginning of a sequence of policy decisions that must be made by the parties.[19] First, the nature of the transfer rights must be determined. In this respect, most transfer systems have provided for preferential hiring exclusively; that is, workers who are displaced from one plant are given priority when applying for jobs at

[18] *Ibid.*, pp. 7–9.
[19] For the greater part, the following discussion of interplant transfer systems is drawn from Arnold R. Weber, "The Interplant Transfer of Displaced Employees," in *Adjusting to Technological Change*, Gerald Somers *et al.*, editors (New York: Harper & Row, 1963).

other plants of the same company. Although the displaced worker's claim to another job is limited, preferential rights can afford a solid opportunity for continued employment when they are applied to a new plant situation where the labor complement has not been filled.

The "transfer-of-operations" principle removes most elements of discretion from the administration of an interplant transfer system. Under this arrangement, employees who are affected by the shift of a particular operation from one plant to another have the unambiguous right to transfer with the operation and the associated jobs. The UAW has entered into over seventy supplementary agreements with General Motors, Chrysler, and Ford implementing the "transfer-of-operations" principle. Transfer agreements also have been negotiated by the Brotherhood of Railway Clerks and at least twenty different railroads, primarily to handle situations involving the consolidation of offices following the introduction of electronic data-processing equipment.

Interplant bumping rights, the strongest form of transfer rights, are rarely found in American collective bargaining agreements. Aside from management's objections that interplant bumping makes it impossible to maintain stability in the allocation of its labor force, union leaders may fear the political consequences of a policy that permits senior workers in one plant to displace junior workers in other plants, especially when the employees involved are members of different local unions. Where interplant bumping rights are established, their application usually is limited by a set of special conditions. A modified form of interplant bumping is found in the sprawling River Rouge works of the Ford Motor Company. This installation comprises fourteen different production facilities, each encompassing a separate seniority unit. Because the rate of displacement varied considerably among the units, the parties agreed to a special program whereby workers with more than fifteen years' seniority who were laid off from one unit could bump workers with less than five years of service in other seniority units of the River Rouge works. Eventually, the seniority gap was reduced to five years when the "bumping" formula was changed to fifteen and ten. The tensions arising from this plan were moderated by the fact that all River Rouge workers are members of the same UAW local. Hence the bumping employee could not be viewed as interloper.

Second, once the nature of the transfer rights has been determined, the seniority of the transferees must be integrated into the seniority lists of the "receiving" plant. Once again, this issue can raise severe conflicts among the different groups of workers with competing claims to the remaining opportunities. Normally, employees who exercise preferential hiring rights are given date-of-entry seniority in the new plant for purposes of layoff, recall, and promotion. Under the application of the transfer-of-operations principle and interplant bumping systems, on the other hand, the transferees usually retain their full seniority.

Third, the initiation of a transfer program inevitably gives rise to the question of relocation and moving allowances. Some form of relocation allowance is prescribed by contracts in the automobile, railroad, meatpacking, and basic steel industries.[20] The most comprehensive benefits are provided in the railroad industry, where the parties have drawn on a large body of past practice in transferring employees between different division and maintenance points of a railroad system. Here all contingencies are covered, from moving expenses to guaranteeing the employee a fair value for the sale of his house.

Fourth, any program for expanding the unit of economic opportunity may involve obligations to train the transferring workers for new occupations, especially if significant differences exist in the methods of production used in the old and new units. In fact, the training requirements posed by transfer programs have not led to any extreme problems of administration. In many cases, the jobs in the new units are sufficiently comparable to

[20] The particular amount of the moving and relocation allowance will vary with individuals. However, most provisions specify some maximum, usually between $500 and $600.

those in the old facilities that the workers can perform satisfactorily after a relatively short break-in period. The experiences in the automobile and meatpacking industries, in particular, indicate that transfer programs can be implemented without imposing heavy training costs. To some extent, the problem has been averted in these industries by maintaining separate transfer lists for craft and production workers. In the petroleum, chemical, and railroad industries, however, special training efforts have been necessary for the successful transfer of employees. On the railroads, displaced clerks have assumed jobs in new data-processing installations after a formal training period that can last as long as six months. Some workers have been unequal to these demands, but in general the promise of a specific job following the completion of the program has provided sufficient motivation.[21]

The implementation of interplant transfer programs has met with varying degrees of success. Although any traveler seeking a motel room after 8:00 P.M. can attest to the fact that Americans are highly mobile, to induce workers to move from plant to plant within the framework of collective bargaining agreements can be a difficult task. The integration of seniority in the receiving plant, the distance between the units, and the nature of the jobs available will all influence the worker's disposition to move. Many of these issues will recede in importance when economic change has been the occasion for the shift in production to a new plant. Nevertheless, where a worker has other options, such as severance pay, even the opportunity to transfer to a new plant may lose its attractions under conditions of uncertainty.

As Chapter 3 will indicate, many of the advantages and problems of interplant transfer systems have been manifested in the Armour experience. Because the cutbacks in employment within the company were precipitous and localized in particular obsolete

---

[21] For a comprehensive discussion of training programs used in internal transfer systems see Richard Beaumont and Roy Helfgott, *Management, Automation and People* (New York: Industrial Relations Counselors, 1964), pp. 131–154. Also see Weber, *op. cit.*

plants, transfer to established or newly constructed units was an obvious device to allocate the remaining job opportunities among the incumbent workers. The first tentative steps taken in this direction in Oklahoma City led ultimately to a highly developed transfer system. But in the process the parties learned, sometimes painfully, that such programs often placed in sharp relief the complex conflict of interests found in any union-management relationship. Attempts to resolve these conflicts without impairing the effectiveness of the program commanded the continued administrative—and judicial—attention of the Automation Fund Committee.

## The Drive for Shorter Hours

While interplant transfer programs represent an innovation, the drive for reducing the hours of work is a venerable issue in American industrial relations. Present-day emphasis, however, is somewhat different from that of the past. Historically, shorter hours have been urged to safeguard the workers' health, increase wages, and protect against seasonal or cyclical unemployment. By contrast, the current demands for a reduction in working hours represent an effort to deal with secular contractions of employment opportunities. Moreover, much of the emphasis has shifted from shortening of the work day to reducing the work year through a variety of measures.

This is not the place for a full-scale analysis of the relationship between operating costs and shorter hours. Suffice it to note that shorter hours as a method of adjusting to technical change, at least in the short run, has been sternly resisted by management on the grounds of cost. In addition, the frequent linking of the demand for shorter hours with a demand for an increase in hourly wages, so as to maintain the previous level of weekly compensation, is not calculated to assuage management's suspicions concerning the union's motives in this area.

In any event, the unions' recent efforts to reduce the hours of work on a daily or weekly basis generally have been unsuccessful. Such achievements to date have been in industries that already enjoy relatively short hours by national standards. Thus, the International Typographical Union in New York reduced the regular hours of work from 36¼ to 35 per week as part of the package that settled the prolonged newspaper strike in 1963.[22] Other modest reductions in the work week have been won in recent years by brewery truck drivers and various groups of construction workers. The most auspicious breakthrough in the drive for shorter hours was made by Local 3 of the International Brotherhood of Electrical Workers in New York City, when building contractors acceded to the union's demand for the 5-hour day. Again, however, the victory was won on a battlefield where the union had achieved conspicuous successes in the past. Local 3 had attained the 6-hour day, 30-hour week more than two decades before. In addition, the relation between the IBEW's triumph and protection against displacement was indirect at best, in view of the manpower shortage that afflicted the New York construction industry at the time the agreement was negotiated. In the succeeding year, approximately 4,000 electricians were attracted to New York from other parts of the country by the promise of steady work and high wages, and were working in the city on temporary permits issued by the union.[23]

Efforts to share employment opportunities through shorter hours have had greater success where the objective has been a reduction in the hours of work per year rather than a diminution of the work day and work week. On this front, the parties have shown considerable ingenuity in devising various forms of compensated leisure. The United Steel Workers has pioneered in the development of the "industrial sabbatical" in the basic steel, can,

---

[22] Joel Seidman, "The Unions' Agenda for Security," *Monthly Labor Review*, June, 1963, p. 636.
[23] For a discussion of experience with the 5-hour day, see Theodore Kheel, "How the Twenty-Five Hour Week Has Worked," in Markham, *op cit.*, pp. 100–106.

and aluminum industries. Although the specific formula varies from industry to industry, these plans commonly include an extended vacation of ten to fifteen weeks every five years for workers who meet prescribed seniority standards. These developments in the metals industries have stimulated other innovations. The 1963 agreement between the American Sugar Refining Company and the UPWA modified the steel pattern to establish a program for "phased retirement." Under the plan, extended vacations are given only to workers who are 60 years of age or older. The duration of the extra vacation increases from four weeks to a maximum of twelve as the worker approaches 65. In theory, the "phased retirement" plan will prepare older workers for retirement while creating additional opportunities for younger workers or a defense against possible displacement. The UPWA initially gave some indication that it would press for a similar program in the meatpacking industry, but never seriously did so.

In addition to these ingenious methods of reducing the annual hours of work, further progress has been made along traditional paths. In many union-management agreements there has been a steady increase in the length of paid vacations available to all employees, or conversely, a reduction in the service requirements necessary to obtain a vacation of a prescribed length. In the brewing industry, where new production methods have cut deeply into employment, regular vacations of six to eight weeks for employees with 20 years or more of service are not uncommon.[24] Four- and five-week vacations also have been negotiated with increased frequency in other industries.

Regardless of the route taken to achieve a reduction in hours, this approach to averting labor displacement poses several operational problems. First, where the pressure for efficiency is great, the anticipated job openings may not be forthcoming as management seeks to operate without additional manpower. Although it is too early to reach any conclusive judgments, such a pattern

[24] For example, vacations up to eight weeks were recently negotiated by the Brewery Workers in Cleveland. *Wall Street Journal*, April 29, 1964.

appears to be emerging in the steel industry. Preliminary reports indicate that the number of new jobs opened up by the extended vacation plan has fallen substantially short of the 20,000 expected when the program was put into effect.[25]

Second, it is not clear that workers—or their wives—prefer increased leisure over money income. The incidence of moonlighting and the apparent appetite of workers for overtime at premium pay may minimize the expansion of job opportunities promised by shorter hours. The use of shorter hours as a springboard to overtime and extra earnings is illustrated by the case of the New York Construction Electricians. The 25-hour week notwithstanding, in 1962 an estimated 50 per cent of the electricians were working an average of one additional hour beyond the "normal" overtime allowed by the contract. Indeed, the union has been obliged to establish a ceiling of 20 hours on the amount of overtime that its members can work each week. Initial projections suggested that the reduced work week would yield approximately 1,600 new jobs. Early experience with the program indicated that only 800 to 1,000 new jobs may be attributed to the new work schedule.[26] Although this failure to realize expectations may be traced, in part, to a slight decline in construction, it is also likely that the use of overtime and employer pressure to reduce manpower requirements have contributed to the discrepancy.

## III. Economic Guarantees and Indemnification

Programs for sharing available employment opportunities, when geared to normal economic processes, embody the expectation—or hope—that incumbent workers can maintain a job within the bargaining unit. Yet the magnitude of displacement

[25] Various officials in the steel industry acknowledge that calculating the "pure" employment effect of the extended vacation is difficult. The measurement problem has also been compounded by the increased employment in the steel industry as a result of the expansion of production.

[26] Kheel, op cit., pp. 104–106.

threatened by technological change may clearly be beyond the capabilities of these programs. In this event, unions in particular are likely to turn to economic guarantees and/or indemnification. Under a system of economic guarantees a group of workers is assured of a job or minimum earnings over a prescribed period of time. The employee preserves a formal connection with the firm, but the link between compensation and actual work is weakened. Where there is indemnification, the connection between the worker and the firm typically is severed. The employee is paid a lump sum and is then forced to move into the labor market beyond the firm.

## Economic Guarantees

To a degree, economic guarantees are subject to the observation that has sometimes been made concerning the guaranteed annual wage: Where it is most needed, it is impractical; where it is practical, it is not needed. Thus a true guarantee of employment or income over a specified period of time can impose staggering costs on management when the need for workers drops substantially below the guarantee level. Where this situation is foreseen, guarantees are not likely to appear. On the other hand, when there is no genuine problem, the union will not exert its bargaining power to win a tin trophy.

In practice, economic guarantees are most likely to emerge under two sets of conditions. First, such guarantees may be established where there is a prospect that they can be honored at negligible or moderate cost. In this situation, the true significance of a guarantee is that it becomes a financial goad to management to engage in systematic manpower planning, involving the full exploitation of attrition to minimize the costs of assurance of jobs or income. The guarantee, in effect, is a safeguard against the contingency that technical change will be introduced without regard to the interests of the labor force.

Second, employment and income guarantees for a limited time

may be accepted by management as the *quid pro quo* for the right to introduce changes that promise substantial improvements in efficiency. Even though the cost of the guarantees is heavy, it is outweighed by the anticipated benefits. The offer of a guarantee may be necessary to overcome union resistance to the modification of work rules that limit management's discretion in the use of new methods. In this sense, economic guarantees are a form of collective indemnification which approach the conventional concept of severance pay.

The indemnification approach, in its own right, avoids most of the complications associated with a continuing attachment of workers to a firm with declining employment opportunities. Instead, measures such as severance pay usually signify a final break in the employee-employer relationship. With a few exceptions, receipt of severance pay also liquidates any right to other benefits provided under the agreement.

Because of the special conditions required, economic guarantees have not been widely used in dealing with the consequences of technical change. Where they occur, they generally have been part of a comprehensive program for handling displacement. The special agreement between the Kaiser Steel Corporation and the United Steel Workers was designed to promote efficiency and to set up incentives for an increase in labor productivity. The heart of the agreement is a formula for sharing the gains of this increased productivity among the workers and the company. However, a critical provision in the plan also stipulates that no employees will be laid off because of improved work methods. Workers who are displaced from their jobs as a result of technical change are placed in an employment pool where they are guaranteed payment for 40 hours of work a week or the average number of hours worked in the plant, whichever is the lesser amount. The initial experience under the plan supports the contention that economic guarantees are most feasible where they are least utilized. In the first nine months of the program, only one worker had been placed in the employment reserve; and he was covered by the protective provisions of the guarantee for only three hours.[27]

Economic guarantees play the same defensive role in the Modernization and Mechanization Agreement between the Pacific Maritime Association and the ILWU. The primary objective of the agreement is to pave the way for the introduction of new methods in the West Coast longshore industry by removing traditional or contractual restrictions on management's authority. In return for these concessions, the PMA agreed to pay $29 million into a special fund that would be used to finance various programs to avert or cushion the economic consequences of these changes upon fully registered, "Class A" longshoremen. Among other things, the proceeds of this "buy-out" could be used for employment and income guarantees. All "Class A" longshoremen were protected against layoffs resulting from new methods of handling cargo. This protection was buttressed by an income guarantee that is payable if the hours worked per week drop below 35 because of "mechanization." As previously indicated, "induced" attrition through early retirement has more than kept pace with the reduction in employment opportunities arising from technical change. Consequently, between 1960 and 1963 the wage and employment guarantees have seldom, if ever, been used.[28]

The contrasting experience of the ILWU in Hawaii provides additional insights into the nature and uses of economic guarantees. Following the West Coast pattern, a mechanization and modernization agreement was negotiated between the union and the Hawaiian shipping companies. The potential labor savings from mechanization were greater in Hawaiian ports than along the West Coast, so that it was not possible to secure a complete

[27] Kossoris, op. cit., p. 33. For a discussion of the achievements and problems of the Kaiser Plan see "The Kaiser Steel-United Steel Workers Long Range Sharing Plan: A Joint Statement of Results During the First Year" (mimeographed, 1964). In this report, the parties indicate that the employment guarantees have not been fully tested and warrant continued close attention.
[28] Fairley, op. cit.

guarantee against layoff. However, a complex set of benefits is applied to those whose economic position might be impaired. Included in the package is a wage guarantee that becomes effective when employment opportunity drops to less than 32 hours per week, averaged over a calendar quarter. The ILWU has considered raising the Hawaiian guarantee to the 35-hour level obtained in the West Coast agreement, but has been reluctant to press this demand because substantial sums already have been paid from the benefit fund under the 32-hour formula. Raising the guarantee to 35 hours would put severe strains on the financial resources available under the agreement to finance other displacement benefits.[29] Even the union must deal with "economic" problems in the allocation of resources among alternative elements of a comprehensive program for dealing with technological displacement.

That the use of economic guarantees is most widespread in the railroad industry is in part a reflection of historical factors. Income guarantees were incorporated in the 1936 Washington Job Protection Agreement negotiated by the major carriers and the railroad unions to handle the dislocations induced by the merger of two or more railroad lines. Building on this precedent, income guarantees have been established in cases of displacement associated with technical change within a single carrier. Typically, the railroad agreements specify that employees who are "adversely affected" are eligible for a "displacement allowance" that provides complete or partial protection of previous levels of earnings. Under the agreement between the Southern Pacific Railroad and the Brotherhood of Railway Clerks, workers displaced to lower-paying jobs suffer no income loss for five years. Similarly, employees who are laid off receive between 60 and 70 per cent of average monthly pay over a five-year period. The allowances are reduced proportionately as an employee's outside earnings approach the income level attained while working for the carrier.[30]

[29] Ibid., p. 43.
[30] Labor, March 23, 1963.

Income protection also was a fundamental concept in the arbitration decision that settled—or gave pause to—the historic Diesel fireman dispute. Firemen with between two and ten years of service could be displaced from existing positions and either laid off or reassigned to "comparable" jobs subject to income guarantees.[31] The potential costs of these economic guarantees in the railroad industry are high. Doubtless management was willing to accept such burdens on the assumption that the cost would be quickly amortized by savings in labor requirements under the new technological conditions.

## Severance Pay and Indemnification

Indemnification through lump-sum severance payments is a terminal step in the adjustment to technical change within the bargaining relationship. In theory, severance pay may contribute in diverse ways to the adjustment process. First, it presumably offers the employee some restitution for the loss of high "property rights" in a job. Second, severance pay provides the displaced worker with resources to meet his financial obligations while canvassing the labor market for a new job. And third, when the aggregate amount of severance pay is substantial and is paid as an out-of-pocket expense rather than on a funded basis, the cost might create a short-term deterrent to the rapid introduction of labor-saving technology.

There is insufficient evidence to support any conclusive evaluation of the relation between the theoretical and practical consequences of severance pay. In any event, severance pay provisions are now found in approximately 30 per cent of the collective bargaining agreements in the United States. Between 1956 and 1963, the percentage of plans including such provisions nearly doubled.[32] Today, termination pay arrangements are widespread

---

[31] "Arbitration Board's Award in Railroad Dispute," *Monthly Labor Review*, January, 1964, pp. 36–43.
[32] Kossoris, *op. cit.*, p. 17.

in most large industries, including automobiles, farm equipment, steel, rubber, aerospace, meatpacking, electrical machinery, communications, and ladies' garments.

In some industries, supplemental unemployment benefits were the precursor of severance pay. SUB plans originally were designed to protect the worker's income against seasonal and cyclical fluctuations in production and employment. Nonetheless, many of these programs have been modified to meet the requirements of permanent displacement and to provide an income stream for varying periods following layoff.[33]

The program that evolved during the life of the Automation Fund Committee fits generally into the pattern of American industrial relations practice: that is, the uncertainties of the meatpacking industry carry with them a high potential cost for any long-term employment guarantees. In addition, the work rules in the industry are not such as to constitute a substantial incentive to management to "buy-out" any real or imagined inefficiencies with safeguards of employment. Consequently, aside from the short-term guarantee implicit in the advance-notice clause governing plant shutdowns, long-range job guarantees have not been forthcoming in the Armour situation. The UPWA announced its intention to pursue this objective at its 1964 convention, but the demand did not come to fruition in the subsequent negotiations with Armour. Instead, the parties have been satisfied thus far to maintain a system of severance pay to indemnify workers who are permanently displaced. In addition, the special Technological Adjustment Pay program provides further income protection to displaced workers awaiting transfer to another plant.

## IV. FACILITATING THE TRANSITION TO THE LABOR MARKET

When labor displacement becomes an irrevocable fact, workers are cast into the labor market to fend for themselves. In fact and

[33] Kossoris, *Ibid.*, pp. 18–19.

theory, the labor market is still the principal mechanism for adjusting to new manpower requirements in the economy. Accordingly, professional economists have found great comfort in the operation of the "invisible hand" in the market place. There is ample evidence, however, that in certain instances this "invisible hand" is all thumbs and in need of guidance by unions and management.[34]

The possible types of guidance are twofold: efforts to facilitate placement with other firms, and occupational retraining. Where such programs have been adopted, they were nearly always extra-contractual. They reflected the willingness of the parties to extend the scope of their obligations beyond the plant gate or union hall, especially when there was large-scale displacement in a short period of time.

## Placement Activities

Direct placement campaigns for displaced workers often must overcome formidable obstacles. Frequently the job-seekers suffer from handicaps identified with race, age, education, and the lack of transferable skills. In addition, the labor market may not be broad and buoyant enough to make it probable that the quest for new employment will end in success. Within these limitations, the parties can make a modest contribution to the adjustment process by collecting and disseminating job information and by counseling job-seekers in the realities of the labor market. Management representatives may actively canvass other employers, while the union can take steps to organize the "grapevine" that functions in every labor market. Another important measure is the initiation of early and active cooperation with the local office of the employment service, which may be geared to handle large groups of displaced workers on a special project basis.

[34] For analysis of the labor market experience of workers displaced by plant shutdown, see Richard Wilcock and Walter Franke, *Unwanted Workers* (New York: The Free Press of Glencoe, 1963).

The results of union-management placement efforts have been highly variable. A combination of loose labor markets and lack of skills on the part of the job-seekers often have imposed basic limitations. In other cases, where the scope of the campaign extended beyond a single labor market and where the workers involved had recognizable, transferable skills, efforts at placement in other firms have had more auspicious results. Thus, the International Association of Machinists attempted to find new employment opportunities for the 4,000 employees of the Republic Aviation Company on Long Island, New York, who were displaced by a plant shutdown. The union reported that it had located approximately 3,000 job openings in various parts of the country and had helped to place one-half of the workers who used its services.[35] Similarly, effective programs have been carried out to find new positions for professional personnel who were thrust into the labor market by the closing of large metropolitan newspapers. And in one heroic instance, the UAW uncovered several job openings in the Swedish automobile industry for workers who became unemployed as a result of the closing of the main Studebaker plant in late 1963.

### Retraining

In recent years, retraining has commanded the increased attention of unions and management as a potentially useful adjunct to placement efforts. Because many of the workers who are most vulnerable to displacement by new technology have minimal or nontransferable skills, retraining can promote occupational mobility and thus re-employment in the labor market. Training programs for jobs outside the bargaining relationship have been initiated by union-management agreement in a few cases. The UAW and the Autolite Company sponsored a special retraining project for workers who were displaced by the shutdown of that company's

---

[35] International Association of Machinists, *Meeting the Problems of Automation Through Collective Bargaining* (Washington, 1960), p. 22.

large installation in Toledo, Ohio. A unique agreement between the International Good Music Company and the IBEW established a trust fund, financed by 5 per cent of the receipts from the sales of automated equipment and program service, for retraining radio and television employees who lost their jobs because of the introduction of these devices.[36] Another agreement, between General Electric and the International Union of Electrical Workers, also makes occupational retraining for jobs outside the firm an option available to displaced workers.

The programs of the Automation Fund Committee have put considerable emphasis on facilitating the adjustment of displaced workers in the labor market at large. In four major plant shutdowns the committee has initiated active placement and retraining efforts. The continued use of such measures by private parties to deal with the consequences of large-scale displacement is probably unique in American industrial relations. These programs took shape before an interplant transfer system and other measures to conserve employment opportunities within the firm had been well articulated. As such, the placement and retraining activities were a recognition that the displaced meatpacking workers had special disabilities in finding new jobs outside Armour. Although other remedial measures have come to play an increasingly important part in the committee's programs, activities aimed at easing the transition to the labor market at large have been accepted as an important supplement in attacking the problems of displacement.

## The Role of Collective Bargaining

This analysis should not imply that any particular collective bargaining relationship follows a fixed pattern in the development of programs to deal with the consequences of economic change. To a considerable extent, the specific tactics adopted by the parties will be determined by traditional policies and the immediate eco-

[36] As cited in Seidman, *op. cit.*

nomic circumstances. Thus the use of shorter hours as a traditional device for coping with cyclical fluctuations in the construction industry gave impetus to using the same practice as a defense against technological change as well. In the petroleum-refining industry, on the other hand, a history of generosity in the area of fringe benefits made "induced" attrition through early retirement an attractive alternative.

The parties also will shift their emphasis as change occurs in the economic environment within which they operate. It is significant that when aggregate job opportunities in the automobile industry contracted sharply in response to market and technological factors, the UAW raised strong demands for reducing the hours of work by controlling overtime. As employment levels have risen along with expanded sales and production, this demand has receded in importance and higher priority has been given to early-retirement provisions. In the Armour case, the establishment of several replacement plants induced the parties to shift the emphasis from measures aimed at facilitating adjustment in the labor market to those that focus on the "management" of normal economic processes and the allocation of job opportunities within broader internal units.

Undoubtedly, unions and companies will continue to experiment with solutions to the problems posed by technological change. This capacity for experiment has been one of the enduring virtues of the American system of collective bargaining. On the other hand, it has been asserted that collective bargaining cannot change the economic climate, that it can only ration the sunshine—or the rain—as the case may be. To some degree this is true. Under a decentralized system of decision-making, the contribution of collective bargaining is necessarily limited by the scope of the units within the control of the parties. It should not be concluded, however, that collective bargaining has or will play only a minor role in adjustments to technological and economic change. Collective bargaining has helped produce a greater awareness of the magnitude of the problem where casual indifference might have prevailed. It has substituted orderly procedures for improvisation. It has sought some acceptable basis for distributing the costs and benefits of the new technology among those who are directly affected. To this extent, collective bargaining has in some cases actually promoted the diffusion of new methods of production. And it has attempted to deal with the difficult questions of equity that frequently have been ignored in previous periods of change.

## Methods of Adjustment: Tactics of Government

Although unions and managements play a vital role in developing programs for adjustment to change, their efforts are inevitably directed to the needs of incumbent workers. Government programs, by contrast, concentrate on those who have left the protected confines of the union-management relationship and who have passed into the labor market at large. Hence, measures initiated by the government to deal with the problems of labor displacement generally have had two major objectives: to provide income during unemployment, and to help place workers in new jobs. The latter objective may be achieved by providing a clearing house of information about available job opportunities and by helping unemployed workers equip themselves for these opportunities through various types of retraining.

## I. SUPPLEMENTS TO INCOME

The system of unemployment compensation was originally designed to provide a financial cushion for workers during relatively short periods of unemployment associated with seasonal and cyclical factors. With the press of current developments, however, unemployment compensation has become part of the arsenal of weapons against displacement arising from economic change. In recent years, short-term amendments have been made to existing legislation in order to meet the heavier burdens arising from long-term unemployment. For example, in 1960 and 1961 Congress enacted the Temporary Emergency Unemployment Compensation Act, which made it possible for the individual states to extend the payment of benefits beyond the normal period permitted by existing legislation.

Notwithstanding these measures to extend the duration of benefits, several deficiencies still exist in the government program. In order to be an effective tool for dealing with the problems of permanent displacement, income supplements such as unemployment compensation must be closely articulated with other programs brought to bear on the same problem area. To achieve this objective, there must be administrative coordination with other private and public measures. Thus, in several cases, the receipt of severance pay by displaced workers has meant disqualification for unemployment compensation benefits. Consequently, an unintended but nonetheless real effect of governmental policies has been to weaken the financial cushion afforded by private benefits. Similarly, under regulations prevailing in several states, a worker who on his own initiative enrolls in an occupational retraining course may not be considered "available for work" and thus runs the risk of disqualification for unemployment benefits. At the same time, the worker who passively accepts idleness and satisfies the *pro forma* requirements of "availability" can collect his benefits without bureaucratic hindrance. Thus, while the unemployment compensation system is crucial to the income of unemployed workers, the legal concepts incorporated in the original legislation may constrain private efforts to deal with the same general problem.

Recent changes in the old age and survivors insurance system demonstrate how the provisions of established programs for income maintenance may be turned to effective use in dealing with the special problems of permanent displacement. The 1961 amendments to the Social Security Act made it possible for men as well as women to draw retirement benefits at age 62, thus adding two contributions to private programs for handling employee displacement. First, it offers the older displaced worker the option of withdrawing from the labor market at an earlier age than otherwise would be possible. Second, it has produced a financial climate in which the private parties have been willing to move more rapidly in the direction of compensated early retirement. By dovetailing the benefits available under private pension plans with the supplementary income afforded by OASI at age 62, several companies and unions have established programs that are limited to those employees who have been forced into premature "retirement" by economic change such as plant closings. Once the principle of early retirement is accepted, the tendency has been to remove the special eligibility requirements associated with particular circumstances and to make early retirement an option available to all workers. Presumably, this extension of the early retirement approach will lead to "induced" attrition, reducing the net displacement when economic change results in a contraction of aggregate employment opportunities within the enterprise.

## II. GOVERNMENT MANPOWER POLICIES

The income supplements available under unemployment compensation and OASI constitute efforts to ameliorate the financial consequences of joblessness or withdrawal from the labor market. At the same time, the federal government has embarked on a new policy which promises to make a more direct attack on labor displacement. Beginning in 1962, the Manpower Development and Training Act has provided substantial public funds for the occupational retraining of unemployed and underemployed workers who lack the personal resources to adjust to changing labor market conditions. This program was reinforced by the Vocational Education Act of 1964, which makes a major federal commitment to the expansion and upgrading of public vocational education facilities throughout the United States. In taking this step, the government has moved into areas generally neglected by private parties, whose energies are normally directed at efforts to protect incumbent workers.

The initial experience with MDTA was disappointing. In the

early stages of the federal retraining program, excessively stringent methods of selection restricted training opportunities generally to those workers with the most easily marketable attributes in terms of age, race, and education. At the same time, unemployed workers who suffered from obvious qualitative deficiencies and who might have profited greatly from a modicum of training frequently were denied this aid as a matter of administrative discretion. Such reluctance to deal with the difficult cases has been overcome to a great extent by the 1963 amendments to the Manpower Act, and by the greater self-assurance derived from wider experience in administering the statute. Significant steps have been taken toward directing government resources to the unskilled and the unschooled, where the returns from such public investment might be the greatest. Concurrently, a tentative endorsement has been given to the principle of government encouragement of geographic mobility. For the first time, unemployed civilian workers may move to new jobs in distant cities with direct financial aid provided by the federal government. Again, this measure fills a gap left by the private parties. In almost all cases, such relocation expenses have been paid only in connection with a move between different plants of the same company.

These changes in federal manpower policy also have been the occasion of new orientation on the part of the United States Employment Service and related state agencies. Thus, the state employment services have made a concerted effort to transform their image and functions from those of an "Unemployment Office" to those of a "Community Manpower Center." This has meant a new emphasis on the intensive counseling of unemployed workers in order to expand their occupational horizons, the systematic collection and dissemination of current information concerning labor supply and demand, and the assessment of long-term manpower trends. At the same time, additional measures have been taken to break down the provincialism that has long characterized the operations of local employment service offices. Expanded clearance procedures and the rapid dissemination of information now make it possible for the employment service to coordinate supply and demand over a broad labor market area. To the extent that the plight of displaced workers may be relieved by systematic labor market information—as contrasted with random, informal processes of search—these developments are broadly constructive. In addition, the development of an "early warning system" has underscored the employment service's willingness to deal directly with situations involving mass layoffs.

By moving into these new areas, the employment service has now become a vital component of any private program to cope with the problems of labor displacement. Through its extensive resources and the obvious economies of scale in the collection and dissemination of labor market information, the employment service can do what no private employer is likely to attempt on an individual basis. At the same time, the employment service itself is heavily dependent upon the cooperation of those private groups which it seeks to aid. If it is to function effectively, information on job vacancies must be forthcoming from individual employers. Similarly, employers must be willing to turn to the employment service as a source of new applicants. Clearly, the area of employment service–employer relations constitutes one in which collaboration between public and private groups may achieve what neither can do alone.

## Programs and Policy Choices

This review of private and public programs for dealing with large-scale labor displacement arising from economic change indicates that there is no single or simple approach to the tasks at hand. Different parties operate in different environments and have varying capacities or comparative advantages in formulating a program responsive to the needs of their situations. In some cases, the sagacious use of normal economic processes can have a powerful remedial effect; in others, some form of employment guarantee may be a feasible incentive for the conservation of job opportunities. Beyond the strategic capabilities of the employers and the unions, additional weight must be given to the different circumstances of individual workers. Some workers have highly marketable skills, and a vigorous placement program can bring them immediate help. Others need the additional aid of retraining, whereas retirement may be the preferred option for older workers confronted by displacement.

It is therefore essential that any remedial program consist of a "package" of possible measures for helping particular individuals or groups. These various options may involve both private and public programs. It is crucial to determine the optimal relationships between what the employer and the union can do and what the government should do in each circumstance. In any case, it is of overriding importance that a remedial program include a broad and diverse package rather than merely a single means for moderating the extent and consequences of displacement. "Bold and imaginative" programs deserve the name only if they can apply a range of specialized remedies to the detailed requirements of each situation.

# 3  Initiating Mobility: The Evolution

## of an Interplant Transfer System

THE program of modernization undertaken by Armour and Company entailed the closing of large, obsolete units and the relocation of production facilities and job opportunities in new geographic locations. To preserve these opportunities for incumbent workers in the closed units, it was necessary to develop a working program for interplant transfer. Such programs have been developed in other industries, with variable results. When Armour employees were confronted with the prospect of mass displacement, there had been no experience with interplant transfers in the meatpacking industry and the parties lacked detailed guides to action. Clearly, in the meatpacking industry above all others, the principals could not be expected to buy a pig in a poke.

A first step, as noted earlier, was a study of the operation of interplant transfer plans in other industries. Although this study did not give a practical blueprint for use in the meatpacking industry, it did show that such plans were feasible, and also sharply identified the problems that were most likely to arise. Shortly after the study was commissioned, the company closed its plant in Oklahoma City, where about 450 workers were employed. This shutdown, which occurred one month after it had been officially announced, was the first such occurrence since the inception of the committee. It took place before any concrete plans or procedures had been formulated for handling such events. The committee responded to the situation with an experimental program to find jobs for the displaced workers in the Oklahoma City labor market. It met with meager success, and a supporting program to retrain the jobless workers was then initiated. This effort ultimately provided help to only a handful of people. Nonetheless, the experiment proved extremely useful to the committee in implementing similar projects in other cities, as will be shown in Chapter 4.

Six months after the plant closed, half of the workers displaced by the plant shutdown were still unemployed. Moreover, in the fall and early winter of 1960 the employment situation in Oklahoma City worsened. The committee then agreed to an extracontractual plan for the transfer of workers from Oklahoma City to a large Armour plant in Kansas City. The details of this plan included a provision for the payment of relocation allowances up to a maximum of $325 per person. On the criticial seniority question, it was agreed that transferees would have the status of new employees for purposes of job seniority and severance pay but would retain full company service for the calculation of vacation pay and other fringe items. On January 3, 1961, letters outlining the program were sent to 304 people, with a request for an answer by January 18. Half of those surveyed, 153 people, expressed an interest in the transfer opportunity. Ironically, the plan was never carried out, since production in the Kansas City plant declined shortly thereafter and layoffs occurred among the incumbent workers in the labor force. Nevertheless, this experience crystallized some of the committee's thinking and helped lay the groundwork for the formal transfer plan agreed to in the 1961 negotiations between the parties.

## The Structure of the Interplant Transfer Plan

One of the important results of the 1961 bargaining between Armour and Company, the Amalgamated Meat Cutters and Butcher Workmen, and the United Packinghouse Workers was the first contractual definition of the rights of employees to interplant transfer when subject to displacement in their original plant. The principle involved at this stage of the relationship was not controversial, although the details of the plan presented many points for hard bargaining. The final agreement established the following provisions governing the crucial items of eligibility for transfer, financial support in transition, and the status of the transferees at the receiving plant:

*Eligibility:* Transfer rights can be exercised by any employee who has more than one year of continuous service, who is under the age of 60 and "has the ability to do the job." It may be noted that workers reaching the age of 60 can select retirement with supplementary benefits as agreed upon in these same negotiations.

*Financial Support during Transition:* Two forms of support are provided for workers selecting the transfer option. During the period between layoff and the start of work at the new plant, potential transferees are assured an income of $65 per week for 26 to 39 weeks, the precise duration to be determined by the seniority of the worker. The actual payment from the company, called Technological Adjustment Pay (TAP), is the difference between the weekly income received by an employee from unemployment compensation or other earnings and $65. To be eligible for TAP, a displaced worker must be under 60 years of age and have a minimum of five years' service with the company. During this transition period, payments also are made to maintain the employee's regular hospitalization and medical benefits.

In the event that a potential transferee declines a job offer, his TAP payments are terminated and the amount contributed for his support during the waiting period is subtracted from his severance pay. If no job offer is made during his total period of eligibility for TAP, he can collect severance pay at the lower rate prescribed by the preceding contract.

In addition to the TAP provisions for income maintenance, it was also agreed that a moving allowance would be paid to help defray the expenses of relocation. The actual schedule of benefits called for payments up to a maximum of $520.

*Status in the Receiving Plant:* A principal issue in the development of the transfer plan focused on the relative seniority of the transferring workers at the receiving plant. This was a point of considerable significance since it was assumed that many of the workers electing transfer would have high seniority in their original plant, and thus might acquire a preferred position in selection of jobs and in any subsequent layoff and recall at the receiving plant. In addition, the length of company seniority has substantial implications for the employee's status under various benefit plans.

The agreement reached through negotiation separated job seniority and benefit seniority. The transferring employee is accorded full rights on the latter, but the former is sharply limited. Transferees can bump only those employees at the receiving unit hired after August 7, 1961 (the approximate date on which this agreement was reached); subsequently they will retain a seniority date of August 7, 1961 or their original date of hire, whichever is earlier, for the purpose of establishing relative job rights in the receiving plant. Thus no individual directly represented at the negotiations can be bumped from his job as a result of the operation of the interplant transfer program. At the same time, the base of job opportunities for possible interplant bumping would be broadened as time went on and as new employees were hired throughout the company. In this way, the parties are able to take advantage of company-wide turnover in handling problems of displacement from plants which ceased operations entirely.

This compromise, involving the separation of benefit rights and job rights, obviously is a direct reflection of the political realities of union life and the resistance of each local union to the prospect of "outsiders" displacing its members from jobs. It should be noted further that the transfer rights are extended only to those plants of the company organized by the same international union that held bargaining rights in the old plant; thus no "cross-bumping" rights are established.

### Experience with Interplant Transfer

The interplant transfer program has now been tested in four situations. The circumstances involved were different in each, but the plan clearly has acquired greater meaning as time has passed and experience has accumulated. The first test came only three months after contract negotiations were concluded, when the company closed a plant in Birmingham, Alabama, employing about 150 workers. While turnover in other plants provided a small number of job openings even by that time, the job seniority status of any transfering employee would have been minimal and virtually identical with that of a new employee. Moreover, the job openings were in distant cities, located mostly outside the South. Under these circumstances, there were limited expectations concerning the number of workers who would select the transfer option. In fact, only three people actually accepted job offers, and of this meager number two shortly returned to Birmingham.

The second test of the transfer program occurred in the summer of 1962, when a much larger plant was closed in Fort Worth, Texas. About 800 out of a work force of 1,100 could be considered prime prospects for the transfer option. Twenty workers expressed an initial interest; only six actually transferred to other plants. Of these, three ultimately returned to Fort Worth. Here again the available jobs were in northern cities, and the seniority accorded by the date of August 7, 1961 did not provide substantial protection against subsequent layoff or afford the transferee much discretion in selecting a job. Nevertheless, some effort was made by the union to publicize the transfer option, and the satisfactory experience of one early transferee was widely publicized through local union channels.

At this point, then, the interplant transfer option had been made available to nearly 1,200 displaced workers and only four had taken advantage of the opportunity. However modest the expectations of the parties when they negotiated the transfer plan, the performance clearly fell far below it!

The third experience with the transfer program, involving workers displaced by the closing of the plant in Sioux City, Iowa, stands in sharp contrast to the first two. It was clear to the members of the Automation Fund Committee that if the transfer plan was to play a meaningful part in the adjustments process, considerable energy and new concepts would have to be brought to bear in the administration of the program. At the same time, the location of Sioux City offered substantial advantages over Birmingham and Fort Worth; the bulk of the employment opportunities open to potential transferees were located in the same general part of the country and within a radius of approximately 250 miles. In addition, the base of job opportunities had been expanded as a result of labor turnover during the two years since the inception of the program. About 400 jobs were now available in other plants organized by the UPWA.

One of the first steps taken by the committee to improve the transfer program was to reduce the potential costs and uncertainty associated with the selection of this option. Even the limited experience in Birmingham and Fort Worth revealed the uncertainty in the employee's mind about how he would fare in his new environment. With large amounts of severance pay at stake, an employee might hesitate to transfer to a distant location if, were he to find conditions unsatisfactory and to quit as a result, he would lose severance pay as well as the time and trouble involved in the move. The committee therefore agreed to experiment with "flow-back rights": A transferring employee could return to home base, without prejudice to his claim on severance pay, within a period of three months after arriving at the new plant. An additional three months would be granted upon any reasonable request. Thus, his potential monetary loss was limited to the deduction from his severance pay of any TAP payments and relocation expenses advanced to him by the company. This experimental provision was extracontractual and was not binding on the parties in any future displacement program.

This change in the structure of the interplant transfer system was accompanied by an increase in the scope and intensity of efforts to publicize and administer the program, especially by the union. The transfer option was discussed in great detail with small groups and at several mass union meetings addressed by top-level union officials. The discussions took place considerably in advance of the actual shutdown of the plant. The union urged its members to give careful consideration to this alternative in determining their individual courses of action following the shutdown. The union also took steps to see that transferring workers were greeted with cordiality, or at least without overt hostility, at the receiving plants.

The choices open to the Sioux City workers, as at the other plants, were (1) for those with the requisite age and seniority, one of the various retirement options; (2) severance pay, which averaged about $3,300 per person, with the prospect of participation in private or public retraining programs at some future time; or (3) interplant transfer to one of twelve plants, although the overwhelming bulk of the opportunities were in five major plants in the Midwest.

The transfer choice itself involved three stages: the initial election of transfer as opposed to the other two possibilities; the acceptance or rejection of a specific job offer made about one month after the shutdown, by reporting or failing to report to work at the selected plant; and the decision to stay at the selected plant or return to Sioux City within six months. As the situation unfolded still another opportunity developed. Two new plants were opened by the company, one in West Point, Nebraska, only 50 miles from Sioux City, and the other in Sterling, Illinois, more than 200 miles to the east. The right to bid for employment at West Point was accorded all former Sioux City workers on the basis of seniority, whether or not they had either taken separation pay or elected transfer as their initial choice. The jobs at Sterling were first made available to workers in any of the plants organized by the Amalgamated Meatcutters, as agreed upon among the parties, and then to former Sioux City employees.

As shown in Table 1, the choice of transfer was exercised by a large fraction of the displaced Sioux City workers, although the numbers of persons selecting this option did not exhaust the available jobs. By June, 1964, one year after the shutdown, 205 displaced Sioux City employees were at work in other Armour

TABLE 1. TRANSFER PATTERNS OF SIOUX CITY WORKERS

| | Preference at Time of Closing (June 1963) | Preference When Asked to Report at Receiving Plant (August 1963) | Preference after Expiration of Six-Month Period and Opening of Two New Plants (March 1964) |
|---|---|---|---|
| Selected transfer to old plant | 400 | 203 | 128 |
| Subsequently took pension or separation pay | (197) | (42) | |
| Selected transfer to new plants | not applicable at the time | not applicable at the time | 106 |
| Originally chose separation pay | | | (44) |
| Retransfer from old plant | | | (33) |
| Preferential hiring[a] | | | (29) |
| TOTAL TRANSFEREES | 400 | 203 | 234 |
| TOTAL WORKERS (SIOUX CITY)[b] | 1,150 | 1,150 | 1,150 |

[a] An additional 29 former Sioux City workers are employed at a new plant opened in September 1964, having moved there on their own initiative but under a contract provision calling for preferential hiring of any displaced Armour worker. Thus, the total number of Sioux City employees working in another Armour plant came to 234, roughly 20 per cent of those displaced, as of about two years after the shutdown.

[b] For information on those who did not transfer and elected to take separation pay or pension, see Chapter 4.

plants and another 29 had found employment in an Armour plant opened in September, 1964. The transfer option had the greatest attraction for men; ultimately almost 25 per cent of those eligible benefited from participation in the program. Seventy-five women initially elected transfer, but few accepted a job at another plant when it was actually offered. In some cases the job offered did not suit the tastes of the female applicant, while in others it was clear that mobility was limited by domestic factors and that the woman would transfer only under special circumstances. But it is clear that the transfer plan did help a significant number of displaced workers in Sioux City, workers who otherwise would have been forced to seek employment in a labor market where prospects were dim.

Drawing on the experience in Sioux City, an equally concerted effort was made to use the transfer program when the large Armour plant in Kansas City, Missouri, was closed. Here about 1,000 workers were affected when slaughtering operations were discontinued in August, 1964. At that time it was hoped that the remaining processing departments could continue to operate, but in June, 1965, these units were also closed, with about 950 workers affected. The same broad options were available to all these workers—that is, separation, retirement, and transfer. In addition to transfer opportunities to existing plants, jobs became available in mid-1964 at three new plants which had an estimated 400 openings. Positions were available for 65 workers in a new beef-slaughtering plant in Emporia, Kansas, about 80 miles away; an additional 75 jobs were created by the opening of a new beef plant in Kansas City itself, and about 250 opportunities developed in two stages of a new hog-slaughtering plant in Worthington, Minnesota, some 300 miles from Kansas City. At Emporia and Worthington, workers throughout the Armour chain could bid for the jobs.

## Initiating Mobility

The timing of these new job openings and the double closing made the transfer process extremely complicated. The availability of jobs at Emporia was announced first, before the formal 90-day notice of the impending shutdown had been given by the company to the union. Thus initial decisions were made before the workers were fully aware of their long-run prospects at Kansas City. Consequently, after the 90-day notice was given, the list was reopened and new bids were accepted for transfers to Emporia. At the same time, another announcement was made concerning the possibilities of transfer to the new plant in Worthington, Minnesota. This plant was scheduled to open about two months after operations had begun at Emporia. To complicate the picture further, additional job opportunities developed in Kansas City when Armour purchased an idle facility from another company. Altogether, the workers facing displacement from the main Kansas City plant had three "new" options to choose from in addition to the positions available in the old, established plants.

In view of the uncertainty as to how the bidding and transfer process would work in practice, a large number of employees placed their names on the list for all of the new plants. An employee could always turn down an actual offer, but if he did not submit a bid initially, he was foreclosed from a particular option. In addition, because seniority was the governing criterion, any individual employee would not know what his real opportunities were until the other, more senior workers had made their choices.

These uncertainties were reflected in the final sequence of offers and acceptances. The Emporia plant opened about one month before the Kansas City shutdown. A total of 345 men from Kansas City and 160 from other Armour plants initially bid for jobs at Emporia. This was far more than the number of available positions. However, as the process worked out, only about one in five actually went to Emporia when a firm offer was tendered. Moreover, some of those who transferred returned to their home plant after trying the new jobs, and were replaced by the next applicants on the list. As a result, every man who had indicated a preference for Emporia had an opportunity to transfer to that plant. In the course of this procedure, 78 workers actually went to Emporia from Kansas City and 50 from other Armour plants. After "flow-back" rights had been exercised, 50 of the Kansas City transferees and 15 from the other company units remained to staff the new facility.

A similar shake-out of applicants occurred in Worthington. As in the case of Emporia, the initial list of applicants included many people who did not move when the moment for action arrived. The number of people involved at each stage of the Worthington transfer process is shown in Table 2 below.

TABLE 2. TRANSFERS TO WORTHINGTON

| Plant | Number on List | | Number Moving | | Number Staying | |
|---|---|---|---|---|---|---|
| | Male | Female | Male | Female | Male | Female |
| Kansas City | 289 | 27 | 50 | 7 | 37 | 5 |
| Others | 259 | 19 | 114 | 4 | 92 | 3 |

As the Worthington transfers were concluded, job opportunities were offered Kansas City workers in existing Armour plants in other localities. By this time, the uncertainties that earlier had led many workers to hedge their decisions had diminished. Thus 57 men bid for jobs in other plants, 55 of these moved when the job offer was made, and 48 were still working at the receiving plant six months later.

The announcement that the balance of the Kansas City plant was to be closed further complicated the transfer process. Some older workers had refrained from transfer initially, with the expectation that the remaining operation would continue. What were their job rights vis-à-vis the earlier transferees—or, for that matter, those working in established plants who had transferred there from Sioux City? The simple application of company seniority provided an easy guide; but the needs of transferees for a measure of continuity in a new environment, and of the company for a measure of stability in its plant working force, also commanded attention.

These issues led to a further development of the transfer plan. Cutoff dates were worked out for each new plant, giving protection to any individual in the work force employed there on or before that date, and serving a function somewhat like that of the August 7, 1961 date for the older plants. At the same time, the relative plant seniority of transferees in any individual plant was established in terms of company seniority. Although the general lines of this development were agreed to by negotiation among the parties, some of the particulars, especially the selection of cutoff dates for the new plants, were not. The public members were asked to establish these dates, their decision to be accepted as an arbitration award.

Fortunately, the number of openings in the new and established plants was more than sufficient to take care of all those who wished to transfer following the second phase of the Kansas City closing. Further, most of those who put themselves on this final transfer list did so with uncertainties removed and with a firm intention of moving. Of 113 on lists for various plants, 87 actually moved when firm jobs offers were made.

Altogether, this complex set of transfer opportunities led to a considerable number of geographic moves, a total of 227 by Kansas City workers and 110 by workers in other plants. In addition, all 75 jobs in the new Kansas City beef plant were filled by workers from the old plant in the same city.

## Problems of Administration

### Procedures for Employee Choice

Implementing the transfer program gave rise to a variety of problems of policy and administration. Basic difficulties in the operation of any transfer plan are the establishment of procedures for the election of a specific transfer opportunity and the dissemination of precise information on which a transfer decision necessarily must be based. From the outset of a transfer operation, it is vital to have a clear specification of the nature of the choices open to the potential transferees. On occasion, the options unavoidably will change in the middle of the program; when this happens, the entire selection procedure is badly disturbed and corrective action often must be taken. For example, at Sioux City the availability of jobs at West Point and Sterling was not determined until October, 1963, whereas the intial set of decisions had been made in June, 1963. When the announcements were made concerning these new—and often preferable—opportunities, most of the transferees were already at work in other plants. Consequently, the entire Sioux City roster, including both those who had transferred and those who had elected separation, was re-surveyed to determine their choices in the light of the new options.

Given a set of stable alternatives, the problem of establishing a sequence for the determination of choice must be resolved. On the one hand, it is important to accord those making such a difficult and important decision ample time to consider fully the alternatives. On the other hand, employees further down the seniority list cannot know the options actually open to them until the more senior employees have made definite commitments. In addition, from the standpoint of efficient plant operation, it is desirable to remove any uncertainty about the composition of the labor force as quickly as possible. The provision of TAP during the waiting period, furthermore, may mean that delay in making a choice carries a cost to the company, while the employee also must assume some financial burden in the sense that he receives substantially less income than he would if he were on the job at a new plant.

The balance struck in the Sioux City situation involved the following sequence: (1) The entire range of available alternatives was made known to all employees, who were asked shortly before the actual closedown to choose among retirement, separation, and transfer. Those who chose to transfer indicated their first three preferences among the plants where such rights could be exercised. (2) A 30-day period was provided following the shutdown, during which those who had initially selected the transfer option could explore opportunities in the local labor market and the company could structure job offers according to the expressed preferences and relative seniority of the employees. (3) At the end of this 30 days, specific job offers were made to individual employees, who then had another 30 days before they were obliged to report to the new plant. Under certain circumstances, an additional 30 days could be granted before the transferee actually went to work. Since the total number of job opportunities available was greater than the number initially interested in transfer, it was possible for the company to make an offer to each employee on the list.

Although the approach developed in Sioux City provides a first approximation of the matching of preferences and openings, it still did not reveal to many junior employees the true choices open to them. These can only be known once the senior employees have actually arrived at the new plants. Indeed, in view of the flow-back rights extended to transferring workers, it may be six months before all uncertainties have been ironed out of the decision-making process. By this time, the junior employee inevitably will have made his choice among currently available options. Certainly the Kansas City experience strained the patience of both the displaced workers and the program administrators.

Another illustration of the type of problem resulting from a delayed choice by senior employees occurred in the staffing of a small secondary plant that continued to operate in Sioux City. Three job openings were available in this unit, and they were clearly preferable since no geographical movement would be necessary. Three senior men claimed the jobs but did not fill them immediately, since all three men were temporarily engaged in dismantling operations at the old plant. Junior employees made choices of other plants on the assumption that these jobs were foreclosed. When the time came for the senior employees to assert their options they all changed their minds, leaving the three jobs unexpectedly vacant. Eventually three employees returned to Sioux City from other locations to take these jobs. To play out the string, this meant, of course, that three other openings formerly foreclosed to even more junior employees were not available.

This complicated sequence highlights the importance of prompt and definite choices by senior workers, and their responsibility to junior employees who have deferred to the principle of seniority.

The frivolous exercise of an initial transfer option by senior employees is thus an act of irresponsibility toward junior workers with a definite desire to transfer. Like so many issues involving seniority, the timing and sequence of choices may involve conflicting interests not only between the company and the union but among the employees as well.

The complicated options resulting from the Kansas City shutdown and the openings at Emporia and Worthington gave further illustration of the problems discussed above. As the process worked out, however, all who wished to transfer to either of the new plants had an opportunity to do so, and the sequence of events allowed choices to be made in serial fashion. Thus, the Emporia plant was largely staffed before offers were made at Worthington, and offers of jobs in the older plants followed those made there. Despite the initial confusion, junior workers were able to make their choices on an informed basis.

## The Nature of the Job Opportunities

Another recurrent set of administrative problems centers on the types of jobs available to transferees and the status of these workers when they arrive at the receiving plant. As already noted, the job seniority of transferees to existing plants cannot be dated earlier than August 7, 1961. Although the passage of time has improved the relative position of such a seniority date, this limitation still has a decided impact upon both the choice of job and the security of employment at the receiving end. The high-seniority transferee typically had attained a preferred occupational assignment, reflecting his age and physical abilities. The sudden drop in effective seniority forced these workers to consider jobs that were more demanding physically, perhaps more strenuous than they could readily handle. For example, a few men who had worked as "checkers," jobs with relatively light physical requirements, were offered positions as "luggers," calling for considerable strength and endurance in carrying heavy sides of beef. In another case, the last job available at the new West Point plant was that of a "shrouder," involving the laborious and monotonous task of attaching a canvas cover to a beef carcass. Because of the great divergence between the task levels of the old and new jobs, it is not surprising that several workers declined to make the transfer final, and returned to a layoff status. At West Point, eight job offers were required to fill one position as a "shrouder."

The seniority policy enunciated in the contract also has led to delicate problems in the definition of a bona fide job offer. Low seniority status means that workers are almost automatically offered the marginal jobs at the receiving plant. Should a job in which there is a high probability of frequent periods of unemployment be considered a bona fide offer? Does a job on a second shift, for which there is some presumption that work will be more variable than on the first shift, meet the necessary standards of a firm job offer?

Beyond these considerations, the continued program of modernization and relocation of facilities by the company raised questions about the expected life of some of the plants in which the openings were located. For example, six displaced Sioux City employees elected transfer to Kansas City, only to find operations at this plant being curtailed sharply one year later. This latter issue, of course, points to the need for long-term planning in connection with operating even a short-term transfer program. In this respect, the Automation Fund Committee has been the vehicle for the transmission of information concerning some of the long-run plans of the company.

A special variant of the job offer issue is that of displaced female employees. The range of jobs in a packinghouse customarily filled by women is limited, and the effects of the new technology and work arrangements in the replacement plants have been to curtail sharply and sometimes to eliminate most women's jobs. At the same time, women are even less likely to change their places of residence than men. Therefore, many otherwise attractive transfer offers are unsuitable for women, and the problem of constructing bona fide job offers for them becomes more difficult, if not more contentious.

Financially the problems of developing job offers for women had a special significance, since women electing the transfer option are eligible for TAP and then for modified separation pay in the event that no offer is forthcoming. This arrangement may offer some incentive for displaced women to select the transfer option initially, less in the expectation of eventual transfer than in the hope of maximizing their termination benefits by parlaying TAP and separation pay. In Fort Worth, four women exhausted their TAP benefits while awaiting an acceptable job offer, and received modified separation pay. Following this experience, 75 women, about half the female component of the Sioux City work force, chose the transfer option at the first stage of the decision-making procedure. When the company made strenuous efforts to furnish job offers, the process inevitably involved contention over the validity of the job being proffered. Ultimately, twelve women did transfer to other Armour plants.

Although the problem of defining a valid job offer arises at the time of initial choice, the experience of the Sioux City transferees with respect to stability of employment at the receiving plant indicates that concern over this aspect of the issue may have been overstated. In the first seven months at their new locations, 60 per cent of the permanent transferees had had no interruption in employment and 83 per cent had a break of only ten days or less. In addition, follow-up interviews with the Sioux City transferees indicated that after an initial period of adjustment, most of them were satisfied with their new jobs and had little cause to regret or "second guess" their original decision to transfer.

## Extracontractual Problems

These questions of administration and policy are accompanied by problems outside the mechanics of the plan, involving the workers and community at the receiving end of transfers. The importance of company and union efforts to organize a cordial reception at the existing plants cannot be overestimated. The move to a new community and a new work situation can often be difficult. When interplant transfers are associated with the displacement of incumbent workers, the transferee may justifiably fear that he will be greeted with resentment at the new plant. Under such circumstances, a systematic effort to integrate the transferees into the receiving plant and community is essential. Once these steps are taken, other displaced workers may view the prospect of interplant transfer with greater equanimity.

Special problems of reception may also arise at new plants, particularly when the move is from an urban to a rural environment—a pattern characteristic of many of the shifts in Armour facilities. Frequently the decentralization of operations and establishment of slaughtering facilities in the livestock-producing areas has meant an urban-rural shift as well. Moreover, there are no established local unions to pave the way for the transferee. In fact, residents of the small local community may resent the preemption of new jobs by strangers. It should be noted that the agreement between Armour and the two unions permits 80 per cent of the jobs at a new plant to be taken by transferees from other Armour units. The remaining 20 per cent can be hired by the company in the local labor market. The availability of housing may bring additional complications, especially when interracial relations are also involved. Because housing may be tight in small rural communities, the arrival of Negroes in areas where they have not lived in any great numbers can present a touchy problem in the management of transfers.

Several of these extracontractual problems are illustrated by the implementation of transfers from Kansas City, Missouri, to Worthington, Minnesota. It will be recalled that this case involved the movement of a sizable group of Negro workers to a previously all-white, rural community of 10,000. Recognizing that special problems might develop, the Automation Fund Committee took explicit measures to cultivate a receptive attitude in the community, or at least to dampen any latent hostility. A three-man co-ordinating team worked closely with business and religious leaders in the town. Cooperation was developed with local real estate agents in order to provide the transferees with an acceptable range of housing opportunities. In general, the shift of the Negro workers to Worthington was carried out with a minimum of tension.

Even when cultures are apparently similar, subtle problems may arise in a move from one community to another. For example, a displaced Fort Worth employee of Latin American extraction transferred to a new plant in another small Texas community but soon returned to Fort Worth. His primary reason was an unwillingness to raise his family in a community where the Latin American population followed rural patterns of behavior alien to the city environment to which he was accustomed.

Aside from such social considerations, certain "bread and butter" problems arose that were not easily solved. Except at Worthington, no special steps were taken to help the transferees find adequate housing. Many of them subsequently reported major difficulties in getting settled. Typically, the married (male) worker would first come to the new community without his family. While seeking permanent housing, he would usually live in a rooming house and periodically commute back to his home city. Each of the transitional measures, of course, imposed significant costs on the worker. Although the labor agreement provided a moving allowance for the transferees, the costs of maintaining two residences and of commuting were not covered by the plan. Consequently, follow-up interviews with the transferees revealed some discontent on this issue. These feelings were heightened because most of the workers who transferred had to take what they considered a loss on the sale of their houses in the home city.

Still another financial complication arose in Iowa. Here the unemployment commission ruled that a worker receiving TAP was not eligible for compensation benefits, thus making the company liable for the full $65 per week stipulated by the labor agreement. Under such conditions, the cost of the TAP program to the company would nearly be doubled. The ruling was later reversed; but the incident shows how events outside the control of the parties can influence the operations of the transfer plan.

The normal problems of administering an interplant transfer system are not insuperable, but their successful resolution must be coupled with four crucial administrative elements: (1) policies and procedures that are sufficiently clear-cut to define the initial transfer rights; (2) procedures that reduce the ambiguity of the available choices as rapidly as possible; (3) at least some flexibility in these arrangements so that adaptations can be made to the unique circumstances of a particular transfer operation; and (4) a commitment by the parties to an active and continuous administrative effort in carrying the program to fruition.

## Distinguishing Characteristics of Transferees

The importance of the interplant transfer within the framework of the committee's program and the concerted effort to make this plan operate in the Sioux City case stimulated the Automation Fund Committee to commission a study of workers' choices between transfer and separation pay.[1] Extensive interviews were conducted with a random sample of 390 of the men eligible for transfer, after the shutdown but before the actual unfolding of the complicated decision-making process. The content of the interview was then related to the subsequent choices of the individual workers.

The results of the study sharpened the understanding of factors influencing worker choice and confirmed many inferences drawn from the committee's practical experiences. "Flow-back rights" clearly were of great importance to the men in Sioux City who

---

[1] The study was conducted by Professor Norman M. Bradburn of the Graduate School of Business, University of Chicago, under the auspices of the National Opinion Research Center.

were considering transfer. Thus, this innovation by the committee appeared to be successful. The workers also were highly sensitive to the limited range of jobs available, and to the presumed vulnerability to layoff associated with their low seniority in the receiving unit. Job security thus appeared to be a major variable. It also was apparent that the location of the jobs, in nearby midwestern communities, helped make the transfer plan more successful than in Birmingham or Fort Worth.

Concerning the personal characteristics of the retrainees, it is interesting to note that the men most involved in social contacts and in city affairs were also the men most likely to move. Apparently they were more confident of their ability to adjust to a new community than those who were socially more isolated. The combination of high seniority and substantial family responsibilities also differentiated the transferees from those taking separation pay. Home ownership, by contrast, was not a deterrent to transfer.

Most surprisingly, the amount of severance pay did not appear to have a decisive influence on the choice, although this finding may simply mean that since in Sioux City employees had the "flow-back" option, those with a claim to substantial severance pay could initially select transfer without liquidating their rights to a large lump-sum payment. In earlier cases there were strong indications that the bird-in-the-hand aspects of severance pay had been more attractive than the long-run benefits of interplant transfer.

## Transfer Choices in a Policy Environment

As the committee accumulated experience with the operation of the interplant transfer system, this plan changed from a *pro forma* aspect of the contract into an important part of a more comprehensive program to mitigate the effects of plant shutdowns on the employees involved. In part, the improvements in the use of the plan reflected the passage of time and the wider job base created by company-wide attrition. In addition, the location of recent plant shutdowns in relation to other units where jobs were available made conditions more favorable for transfer.

Clearly the transfer plan, even at its most successful, is no panacea for the problems associated with employee displacement. Under the most favorable circumstances it is apparent that many people still prefer to take their chances in the local labor market rather than move to a strange environment. On the other hand, the opportunity to transfer, where the plan is structured with care, will be seized by a substantial margin of workers. The beginning of wisdom in dealing with major problems of displacement is an appreciation that an over-all solution will emerge only as the product of a number of more limited efforts.

The committee's willingness to adapt to new circumstances, and to increase its administrative effort, were important in improving the operation of the transfer plan. There is little doubt of the positive influence of the "flow-back" provision. More significant, however, was the improved policy framework within which individual choices were made. In the early cases, little was done to stimulate discussion among the employees of the transfer option and to formulate a detailed plan for carrying out the program. In Sioux City and Kansas City, on the other hand, the transfer plan was given great emphasis, and employees could be confident that the plan would have the continued attention of the union and the company. Individuals would not be left to decide on the basis of fragmentary information, or to fend for themselves in a new and hostile environment. Instead, positive and well articulated policies were gradually developed which served as an essential ingredient to intelligent individual choice.

# 4 Financial Cushions: Severence Pay and Retirement Income

THOSE workers who, by choice or necessity, did not participate in the interplant transfer program were left with two alternatives: they could seek other employment or withdraw from the labor market. Either move was likely to mean financial strain or distress for the employee. In order to deal with this exigency, the agreement between Armour and Company and the two meatpacking unions provided for benefits that would cushion the financial shock of either course of action. Thus as is now increasingly prevalent in American industry, many of these workers who faced displacement had the additional options of exercising a claim to retirement income or of accepting a separation pay allowance.

As the earlier discussion of policies for dealing with large-scale displacement suggests, severance pay plans may reflect a diversity of motives and assumptions. On the one hand, trade unions have pressed for separation pay on the grounds that a worker who is involuntarily displaced should be compensated for the loss of "property rights" in his job. This concept has been implicitly accepted in plans that link the amount of severance pay to the length of the employee's service with the firm and his previous level of earnings. Clearly, workers who have been employed for a long period of time in the top rungs of the wage structure have more to lose than their short-time brethren in less well paid positions.

Added to this notion of equity are the realities of the labor market. For displaced workers who have had a long-term attachment to a particular job or industry, finding new employment may not be easy. Thus severance pay affords the worker some additional financial resources so that he can canvass the labor market systematically without a sharp reduction in his standard of living. At the same time, severance pay usually serves a legal and tactical function for the employer. The displaced worker who accepts severance pay generally foregoes any claim to other benefits that may be incorporated in the labor-management agreement.

Private pension plans also have become commonplace in American industrial relations since World War II. They have not been designed to deal with the problems of labor displacement, but rather to assure the worker a continued flow of income when his earning capacity is diminished because of age. Most of these programs are supported by employer contributions to a special fund, from which payments are made when a worker meets specified age and service requirements. To some extent, pensions may be viewed as deferred income set aside for future distribution within the framework of an insurance system.

Although most pension plans are founded on broad considerations of worker welfare, they may also be adapted to programs for dealing with labor displacement—that is, the eligibility requirements may be altered to permit earlier receipt of pension payments. Similarly, the benefit schedule may be adjusted to take into account the transitional needs of workers whose attachment to the firm has been prematurely severed. By instituting such modifications, pension plans can help to facilitate the withdrawal from the labor market of older workers, who often encounter the most difficult problems of adjustment following layoff, and who in any case could then choose from a wider range of alternatives.

## Severance Pay: Benefits and Uses

A severance pay plan was incorporated into the master agreement between Armour and Company and the two major meat-packing unions in 1949. The provisions of the plan are relatively straightforward and have been the cause of only minor disputes. Except for an upward revision in the benefit schedule and the coverage of workers laid off for two years, the plan has been unchanged since its initial inclusion in the labor contract.

To be eligible for separation pay, an employee must meet two conditions. First, he must have had one or more years of continuous service with the company, measured from the time he acquired seniority rights in a particular department. Seniority rights, in turn, are acquired when a new employee has worked a total of fifteen days within a period of thirty consecutive calendar days. Second, the employee must be permanently laid off or on layoff for two years "because of a reduction in forces arising out of the closing of a department or unit of business, or as a result of technological change."

Severance pay benefits are specifically denied those workers who are discharged for cause, who quit voluntarily, or who are laid off as a result of normal adjustments in the size of work gangs. In addition, an employee may be disqualified for separation pay if he refuses an offer of alternative employment by the company in another department or unit of business that is "reasonably accessible to the location of the place of employment from which [he] is being dropped from service." However, the displaced employee is given the option of refusing any alternative job which would mean a decrease of more than 15 cents from the wage rate he has received at his last job with the firm.

The benefits payable under the plan are determined by the displaced worker's regular rate of pay for 40 hours per week and the duration of his employment with the company. A graduated formula is used so that long-service employees will receive proportionately greater benefits than those who have been with Armour for a relatively short period of time. The exact amount of separation pay that may be drawn in any particular case is determined by the following schedule:

Employees with one to ten years of continuous service receive one week's pay for each year of service.

Employees with eleven to twenty years of continuous service receive one week's pay for each of the first ten years and one and three-quarters weeks' pay for the remaining years of service.

Employees with twenty-one years or more of continuous service receive benefits for the first twenty years in accordance with the schedule described above. For each year of service in excess of twenty, a displaced employee will receive two weeks of pay.

The contract permits the employee some discretion in the method of payment. An employee entitled to a separation allowance greater than four weeks' pay may elect to receive his benefits as a lump sum or in installments spread over a specified period of time. Those with a claim to less than four weeks' pay must accept settlement on a lump-sum basis.

## The Distribution of Severance Pay

The implications of this benefit formula are simple and direct. That is, considerable variation in the amount of separation pay might be expected among individual workers and at the different plants, depending upon differences in length of service. Because the wage spread among blue-collar workers is relatively narrow, variations in the regular rate of pay have had a limited impact on the over-all distribution of severance payments. In addition, the fact that a majority of the work force is normally included in unskilled and semiskilled job classifications also reduces the influence of wage differences on the range of separation benefits.

As shown in Table 3, there was a wide dispersion in the

TABLE 3. DISTRIBUTION OF SEVERANCE PAY IN FOUR CITIES

| | City and Number of Employees | | | | |
| | | | | Kansas City (First Layoff) | Kansas City (Second Layoff) |
| Severence Pay | Oklahoma City | Fort Worth | Sioux City | | |
|---|---|---|---|---|---|
| Under $1,000 | 147 | 129 | 418 | 351 | 51 |
| $1,001 to $2,000 | 225 | 280 | 368 | 213 | 182 |
| $2,001 to $3,000 | 59 | 293 | 134 | 39 | 220 |
| $3,001 to $4,000 | 25 | 39 | 46 | 6 | 86 |
| $4,001 to $5,000 | 6 | 24 | 14 | 6 | 12 |
| $5,001 and over | 2 | 10 | 9 | 15 | 10 |
| Average Payment | $1,443 | $2,840 | $2,245 | $1,080 | $2,675 |

amount of severance pay received by particular individuals and the average level of payments made at the different plants. Specific payments to individuals ranged from $100 to $7,000. The average separation payment varied from a little over $1,000 in the first Kansas City layoff to nearly $3,000 in Fort Worth. In gross earnings these benefits were roughly equivalent to nine weeks per employee in the former city and twenty-four weeks in the latter. Although each employee had his own needs and circumstances, the general level of payments appeared to provide a substantial financial cushion against the initial shock of displacement.

Almost all those workers who selected the separation pay option also chose to receive their benefits in a lump sum rather than in installments. This choice was made even though in many cases a displaced worker could reduce the amount of income tax payable on the separation allowance by distributing the benefits over two calendar years. When layoffs occurred toward the end of the year, as in several instances in Fort Worth, only a brief period of restraint was necessary to realize this tax saving.

The reluctance to elect installment payments apparently stemmed from a combination of practical and personal factors. Many of the displaced workers had outstanding debts that demanded their immediate attention. For others, the prospect of receiving a sizable amount of money in one lump sum proved irresistible. When one worker was asked why he elected a lump-sum payment of $2,000 instead of deferring the receipt of part of the allowance for two months and a new calendar year he replied, "Because I've never had that much money at one time before." As will be shown subsequently, this preference does not mean that severance pay is viewed as a financial bonanza for dissipation through extravagant consumption.

Aside from the form of the separation allowance, for the displaced Armour workers there were also problems arising from the relationship of severance pay to other benefits that might be claimed under the law. The great majority of the workers had sufficient work experience so that when they were laid off they could file for unemployment compensation benefits. To qualify for these, a worker could not receive any wages. If separation pay was considered "wages," the displaced worker could not draw unemployment compensation until the payment was legally "exhausted" by artificially prorating the total amount over the number of weeks used for the initial computation of the separation benefit. Although most industrial relations specialists distinguish severance pay from "wages," authorities in Oklahoma and Iowa ruled that the two categories of compensation were indistinguishable, and disqualified former Armour workers from unemployment benefits until the specified number of weeks had elapsed.

This ruling was eventually reversed in Iowa but remained in force in Oklahoma. As a result, a displaced worker who had used his separation pay to liquidate debts on the assumption that he could draw unemployment compensation to cover current living expenses might find that he had no income at all during the extended waiting period. Clearly, public and private programs in this area worked at cross purposes, undermining the effectiveness of each. In most states, fortunately, this inconsistency has been avoided.

## Severance Pay and Worker Choice

The severance pay provision included in the labor-management agreement is part of a more comprehensive set of measures designed to deal with the problems of labor displacement. After the announcement of an impending plant shutdown a worker may have the opportunity to choose among three mutually exclusive alternatives: severance pay, interplant transfer, and a pension. The options selected will obviously send displaced workers down different economic paths. Presumably, the individual worker will be able to assess his own circumstances and to select whatever option best serves his self-interest and preferences. However, because the immediate returns from each alternative may differ significantly, a worker may make a choice that promises the greatest short-term benefits, while ignoring its long-run implications. Specifically, the possible conflict among available alternatives has been most likely to involve the immediate attraction of severance pay in relation to the long-run benefits of interplant transfer.

Most of the displaced workers who were eligible for some form of pension selected this option—in preference to a separation allowance. In contrast, the large majority of workers who were not eligible for pensions choose severance pay rather than interplant transfer. This choice was made in the face of strong evidence that continued employment with Armour would mean greater returns to the worker than the income that could be obtained in other employment plus the value of the severance payment—and this after a relatively short period of time.[1] Accordingly, it may be suggested that the glitter of a lump-sum separation allowance rendered some displaced workers insensitive to the comparative advantages of other options.

Obviously, many reasons contribute to the decision to accept severance pay rather than transfer. As shown in the preceding chapter, the degree of job security at the new plant, the distance of the move, and related administrative factors clearly influenced the attractiveness of the transfer option in relation to severance pay. As both a theoretical and a practical matter, it is difficult to isolate the impact of separation pay *per se* on the individual's decision. Nonetheless, some inferences may be drawn from evidence concerning the attitudes and behavior of the displaced workers.

First, the explanations offered by those who accepted severance pay may suggest the extent to which the prospect of a large lump-sum payment conditioned the displaced workers' choice. One year after the shutdown of the Fort Worth plant, a sample of 155 men who had elected separation pay were asked why they had chosen this alternative rather than interplant transfer. Aside from those who cited questions of eligibility for transfer, the major reasons

[1] A detailed discussion of the economic experience of former Armour workers in the labor market is presented in Chapters 5 and 6.

involved an unwillingness to leave Fort Worth and the uncertainties surrounding conditions at the new plant. In other words, the negative factors associated with interplant transfer appeared to have a greater impact on the employees' decisions than the lure of separation pay. However, about one-fifth of the respondents did indicate that severance pay, by itself, had an important effect on their choice. These employees viewed the separation allowance as a "good deal," or as a tempting opportunity to liquidate heavy debts, or to set up an independent business, or simply to get out of the meatpacking industry.

Another survey conducted immediately after the closing of the Sioux City plant yielded similar results. Again, the negative aspects of interplant transfer loomed largest in the decision to accept severance pay. On the other hand, about 10 per cent of the workers, a smaller proportion than in Fort Worth, gave heavy weight to the intrinsic lure or "liberating" effect of the separation allowance. Thus, to the extent that credence can be given to the workers' explanations of their actions, severance pay by itself exercised a strong pull on a relatively small proportion of the displaced employees. Instead, the attractiveness of this alternative was generally derived from the shortcomings and uncertainties of interplant transfer.

Second, the effect of separation pay on the displaced workers' decisions can be inferred from the record of the actual choices made following the shutdown. That is, if employees eligible for large lump-sum payments were less likely to choose interplant transfer, the suggestion that severance pay does exercise a strong influence would be revived, notwithstanding the displaced workers' explanations for their actions. The relation between the size of the severance pay to which an employee was entitled and his decision to accept interplant transfer can be assessed indirectly by examining seniority and the interplant transfer experience. Since the severance pay provision in the labor agreement relates the size of the benefit to length of service, variations in seniority will clearly reflect differences in the magnitude of the potential lump sum. Because of the compression of the wage structure in a meat-packing plant, the error introduced by the failure to incorporate differences in rates of pay is limited.

The relation between seniority, as a proxy for severance pay, and experience under the interplant transfer program in Sioux City is presented in Table 4 (A and B). The displaced workers have also been classified by three age groups to reveal more sharply the influence of seniority and thus of severance pay. The data included in Table 4 (A) do not support the contention that

TABLE 4. EFFECT OF SENIORITY AND AGE ON TRANSFER

| | A. *Per Cent Initially Choosing Transfer* | | |
| | | Seniority | |
| Age | Less than 10 Years | 10–14 Years | 15 years or longer |
|---|---|---|---|
| Under 35 | 26 | 41 | ᵃ |
| 35–44 | 37 | 44 | 70 |
| 45 or older | 28 | 38 | 38 |
| | B. *Per Cent Actually Moving* | | |
| Under 35 | 18 | 31 | ᵃ |
| 35–44 | 26 | 25 | 40 |
| 45 or older | 16 | 27 | 17 |

Number of people in study = 389.
ᵃ Case base too small to percentage.
Data from study by Professor Norman Bradburn.

the workers facing the prospect of permanent layoff have been blinded by the glitter of severance pay. On the contrary, within each age category greater seniority is associated with a higher proportion of employees initially choosing interplant transfer. Despite the rise in possible separation benefits, the senior worker was more likely to give serious and positive attention to the transfer option.

As shown in Table 4 (B), the strong positive relation between size of severance pay and interplant transfers is somewhat less when the analysis is extended to those who have actually moved. However, the differences between high and low seniority workers are still significant in each age category. The only important reversal of the relationship was found among those who were 45 or older and who had fifteen years or more of service. Many of these older, high-seniority workers originally selected interplant transfer in the expectation that they could use their seniority to claim a job at the new Armour plant in nearby West Point, Nebraska. When these jobs weren't available during the first round of the selection process, many of the older workers shifted their choice from transfer to severance pay.

Two other incidents during the administration of the Automation Fund Committee's program in Sioux City reinforce the judgment that severance pay did not exercise an inordinate influence on the displaced workers' decisions. It will be recalled that employees who transferred had the right to return to Sioux City within six months and collect their severance pay. Most of the workers who actually exercised this "flow-back" right were young, low-seniority workers, who subsequently collected relatively small separation allowances. It is apparent that their decision to quit the firm was largely determined by dissatisfaction with conditions at the receiving plant.

In another incident, the jobs at the new unit in West Point were finally made available to former Sioux City employees following the resolution of the union-management controversy over this issue. By this time the initial round of decisions had been made and, as indicated previously, some workers had elected separation pay when they couldn't transfer to the new plant. By the terms of the special agreement, all former Sioux City employees, including those who previously had received severance pay, could bid for the West Point jobs. Accepting a job offer at the new plant meant that any severance pay would have to be returned to the company in installments. Despite this condition, approximately 10 per cent of the former recipients of severance pay bid for the new jobs. When the character of the transfer opportunity changed, the attractiveness of the immediate rewards of separation pay was diminished.

On the whole, it does not appear that severance pay distorts the worker's ability to select the adjustment option that is in his own interest. In the context of the Automation Fund Committee program at least, the choice of separation pay seemed to reflect the special circumstances of the workers and the relative attractiveness of other alternatives. This is a matter that can best be considered within the framework of a comprehensive program. The widespread selection of separation pay is likely to indicate deficiencies in other options rather than economic myopia on the part of the displaced worker.

## The Uses of Severance Pay

Although the demand for indemnification for the loss of "job property rights" is usually a central argument in the negotiation of severance pay plans, the primary function of such provisions is to afford transitional income to the displaced worker who is seeking a new niche in the labor market. Information concerning the uses of severance pay by the recipient can shed some light on the extent to which this objective is realized. There is a presumption that the displaced worker will exercise prudence in his expenditures and will resist the temptation to use these funds for extravagant consumption. Even though one man's "prudence" may be another man's "extravagance," it would appear that the recipients of severance pay were generally prudent in their expenditures. Where those expenditures were inconsistent with the notion of transitional income, the reasons for the deviation usually have been outside the worker's immediate control.

Table 5 presents general data concerning the uses of severance pay by a sampling of displaced Armour workers in Fort Worth and Sioux City. The respondents were asked to classify the use of severance pay by magnitude and category of expenditure. Magnitude was specified in qualitative terms—"most of the severance pay, quite a bit of it, a little or none of it." The substantive categories covered payment of debts, living expenses, "something

TABLE 5. USES OF SEVERANCE PAY: FORT WORTH AND SIOUX CITY
(IN PER CENT OF RESPONDENTS)

| Use/Amount | Fort Worth | | Sioux City | |
|---|---|---|---|---|
| | Men | Women | Men | Women |
| *Debt Payment* | | | | |
| Most or quite a bit of it | 59 | 43 | 61 | 47 |
| A little of it | 8 | 9 | 12 | 14 |
| None of it | 33 | 48 | 27 | 40 |
| *Living Expenses* | | | | |
| Most or quite a bit of it | 40 | 43 | 34 | 45 |
| A little of it | 13 | 13 | 22 | 10 |
| None of it | 46 | 44 | 44 | 45 |
| *To Buy or Do Something* | | | | |
| *I Always Wanted To Do* | | | | |
| Most or quite a bit of it | 19 | 4 | 16 | 10 |
| A little of it | 10 | 9 | 18 | 17 |
| None of it | 71 | 87 | 67 | 72 |
| *Savings* | | | | |
| Most or quite a bit of it | 18 | 22 | 13 | 21 |
| A little of it | 22 | 40 | 12 | 3 |
| None of it | 60 | 39 | 75 | 76 |

Fort Worth
Number of men in sample=155
Number of women in sample=23

Sioux City
Number of men in sample=131
Number of women in sample=29

you always wanted to buy or do," and so on.

The survey revealed that the majority of the workers in both Fort Worth and Sioux City used most of their separation allowance to pay off debts. Indeed, some of the individual workers reported that they had "never seen" their severance pay because it was immediately claimed by various creditors. The extensive use of separation allowances for repayment of debts reflects the dramatic change in the economic status of the worker as a result of being laid off, rather than any improvident behavior. That is, many of the workers had regularly borrowed from the company credit union while they were employed. Normally, these loans would have been repaid in installments over an extended period of time. However, when the plant was shut down and the workers were displaced, the credit union required immediate repayment in full wherever possible. For many workers this constituted a relatively large claim on their separation pay. In addition, the worker's other creditors, if any, also were likely to appear on his doorstep to demand the outstanding balance.

The heavy burden of debt helps to explain why such a large proportion of the workers—about 45 per cent—reported that they had used none of their separation allowance for living expenses. Many had no funds left for this purpose after satisfying creditors. On the other hand, 35 to 45 per cent of the workers sampled also stated that they had used most or "quite a bit" of their allowance to meet living expenses. Where some money remained after paying debts it was likely to be used for meeting regular financial obligations.

There is little evidence that the recipients of severance pay spent it wastefully. A relatively small proportion used the money for "something they wanted to do or buy." Indeed, about as many workers saved some portion of their severance pay as used it for a major purchase of this nature. Moreover, the long-term desire was more likely to be for a washing machine or the down payment on a business than a trip to Hawaii or a new sports car. These findings are reinforced by those for both Fort Worth and Sioux City, which show the same pattern.

Some distinctions between men and women may be noted in the use of severance pay. Women were less pressed than men by the need to repay debts, and in general showed a slightly greater tendency to save a portion of their severance pay. This difference is consistent with the observation that many of the women were secondary wage-earners in the family, and that their displacement did not have as profound an effect on domestic finance as that of the male breadwinners. It must be conceded, however, that the apparent restraint of women from using their severance pay for something they wanted to do or buy runs counter to the usual assessment of feminine spending habits.

For the greater part of the displaced Armour workers, it appears that severance pay served as a "financial cushion." But, because so many of the workers had to use a large portion of the allowance for repayment of debts, the resources available for everyday living expenses were less than might have been expected. It may be contended that debt reduction is an essential step in the adjustment of the displaced worker to his new circumstances, so that severance pay still performs an important function. Although this contention may have some validity, it should also be recognized that the attrition of severance pay by repayment of debts undoubtedly reduces the time open to the worker in choosing a new course of action in the labor market.

*Severance Pay and Labor Market Experience*

Even though the "financial cushion" is reduced by repayment of debts, severance pay still provides the unemployed worker with an extra margin of resources. With it, the job-seeker may carry out a more systematic canvass of the labor market, and may wait until an attractive opportunity comes along. Or, to reverse the chain of causation, severance pay may reduce the immediate pressure for new employment so that the displaced worker simply stays out of the labor market for a longer period than he could otherwise tolerate. In either case, differences in the amount of severance pay received may be reflected in variations in the time elapsed between layoff and obtaining the next job. If the worker has used this time to explore the labor market, additional variations may be found in the wages on the initial job.

Only fragmentary data are available on the relation between the severance pay and the labor market experience of the displaced workers. Table 6 shows the broad relationships between the amount of severance pay received and the length of time following layoff and before obtaining the next job. The data are drawn from a sample of male workers in Fort Worth and Sioux City who did not enter a retraining program. Some differences may be observed between those workers who received moderate and relatively large separation allowances. Thus, in Fort Worth 86 per

TABLE 6. SEVERANCE PAY AND TIME ELAPSED SINCE LAYOFF AND
BEFORE NEXT JOB (MALES)

| Severance Pay | Per cent in each severance pay category finding first post-shutdown job within five months | |
| --- | --- | --- |
| | Fort Worth | Sioux City |
| Less than $1,000 FW, N=15 SC, N=54 | 86 | 80 |
| $1,000–$1,999 FW, N=46 SC, N=47 | 56 | 72 |
| $2,000 or more FW, N=39 SC, N=21 | 46 | 67 |

cent of those who claimed less than $1,000 in severance pay were
employed again within five months after layoff. On the other
hand, only 46 per cent of those receiving severance pay in excess
of $2,000 had found or accepted a new job in the same period.
The relationship is similar for Sioux City, although the difference is
less than at Fort Worth.

Further analysis was made of the wages paid on the next job to
determine whether the longer period of unemployment or job-
seeking was associated with higher wages, once employment was
found. In fact, no differences were apparent. Substantially the
same distribution of wage rates was noted for workers with high
severance pay and a relatively long period of unemployment as
for those with a modest separation allowance and a short period
of unemployment. As a first approximation, the longer waiting
period associated with higher severance pay was not translated
into better economic performance in the labor market.

These findings raise more questions than they answer. The
difference between the size of separation pay and the duration of
unemployment or job seeking may be explained entirely by the
fact that those receiving a large allowance were also older and
could expect to encounter greater difficulty in finding new jobs.

But if so, why wasn't the age handicap further reflected in differences in the wages of those receiving large and small amounts of severance pay? Beyond these considerations, the experience of particular workers was surely influenced to some degree by present indebtedness, skill level, eligibility for unemployment compensation, and a variety of other, related factors. Unfortunately, the limitations of the data and the size of the sample preclude any meaningful analysis of these questions at present.

The absence of precise information perhaps highlights a general deficiency in the use of separation pay as part of an over-all program to deal with large-scale labor displacement. To be sure, separation pay provides some immediate financial comfort to the workers, at the same time that it satisfies the demand for "equity" in compensating them for the loss of their jobs. Nonetheless, if separation pay plans are to be meaningful in private manpower policies, more information must be available to determine how, if at all, they affect the behavior and fortunes of the worker when he has left the confines of the union-management relationship. Indeed, once such information is at hand, changes may be required in the nature and administration of the severance pay plans themselves.

## Retirement Income

For the older worker, partial or complete withdrawal from the labor market is often the appropriate response to a plant shutdown. Because he does not have the right to interplant transfer,[2] or because he is unwilling to move to a new city, continued employment with the firm is not a real alternative. At the same time, the probability of re-employment at a wage equivalent to that received at Armour—or even at a substantially lower wage—must be rated as small. In most cases, however, the actual feasibility of withdrawal from the labor market under the abrupt cir-

[2] It will be recalled that under the terms of the labor agreement in effect at Armour, transfer rights are not extended to workers over 60 years old.

cumstances of a plant shutdown will be determined by the availability of retirement income of some sort.

The agreement between Armour and Company and the two meatpacking unions contains three different options for the retirement of workers who meet the specified conditions:

*Normal Retirement* can be elected by those employees who are 65 years of age or more and who have completed at least ten years of service. Under this plan, the retiring employee received monthly payments equal to $2.50 for each year of credited service.[3] Most of those workers eligible for normal pensions would have retired before the particular plant shutdown. However, this option still had specific applicability to those who were over 65 and still working. The labor agreement provides that employees who were 60 and over on January 1, 1960 must retire at age 68. Those who were under 60 on January 1, 1960 must retire at age 65. Therefore, normal retirement will have no significance as an adjustment measure in the event of plant shutdowns after January 1, 1968.

*Early Retirement* as an option for male employees who are over 60 and less than 65 years of age and who have at least ten years of service. Female employees may choose early retirement at age 55. Benefits are calculated on the same basis as normal retirement except that they are reduced by .5 of 1 per cent for each calendar month by which the employee is under 65 at the date of his early retirement. Thus, monthly pension payments to a man retiring at age 60 will be 30 per cent less than normal retirement benefits, while a woman's pension may be reduced as much as 60 per cent if she retires at age 55. Obviously, early retirement may diminish considerably the current retirement income of a displaced worker who selects this option.

*Special Retirement* is the major modification of the company pension plan made in 1961 in response to the unique requirements of a plant shutdown. Any worker who is displaced as a result of the closing of a plant or a major department, who is 55 years of age or older, and who has twenty or more years of service, may receive a special pension. The amount of the monthly pension benefit is 1½ times the sum that would be payable under the normal retirement

[3] Beginning January 1, 1965, the pension formula was changed to $3.25 per month for each year of service.

plan. In effect, those who collect the special pension receive $3.75 per month for each year of service instead of $2.50 per month.[4] This "1½" pension is continued until the employee reaches age 62 or becomes eligible for retirement or disability benefits under the Federal Social Security system, whichever occurs first. At that time, the pension payments by the Company drop down to the "normal" benefit level of $2.50 per month for each year of service. In this manner, the special retirement plan aims at bridging displacement and Social Security eligibility for older, long-service employees. Otherwise, the male employee between 55 and 60 years of age would have no pension option at all, while one between 60 and 65 could only choose reduced benefits under the early retirement plan. An important distinction was made between voluntary early retirement and the premature retirement occasioned by a plant shutdown.

The experience with the three retirement options in five cases is presented in Table 7. Several observations may be made on the basis of these data. First, although pension benefits undoubtedly were important in individual instances, their over-all contribution to the program for adjustment to plant shutdowns was only modest. In four of the closings the proportion of the displaced workers receiving retirement benefits was less than 10 per cent and was as low as 2 per cent in the Oklahoma City situation. However, in the second Kansas City layoff nearly one out of five of the workers claimed some form of retirement benefits.

The differences in the contribution of retirement benefits to the program for adjustment to displacement will, of course, reflect differences in the proportion of the plant work force that is eligible for this option in each case. The number of persons eligible, in turn, will be determined by the age and seniority characteristics of the employees—considerations that are not subject to administrative discretion. In Sioux City approximately 18 per cent of the work force was eligible for some form of retirement option while in the second Kansas City layoff about 30 per cent fell into that category. Clearly, this difference contributed to the variable im-

[4] As of January 1, 1965, the special pension was increased to $4.875 per month for each year of service.

TABLE 7. EXPERIENCE WITH RETIREMENT OPTIONS IN FIVE CASES

| | | | | City and Number of Employees Eligible and Selecting Option | |
| Option | Oklahoma City | Fort Worth | Sioux City | Kansas City (1st layoff) | Kansas City (2nd layoff) |
|---|---|---|---|---|---|
| *Early retirement* | | | | | |
| Eligible | 38 | 97 | 112 | 17 | 117 |
| Selected option | 5 | 27 | 48 | 16 | 98 |
| *Normal retirement* | | | | | |
| Eligible | 8 | 17 | 8 | 25 | 41 |
| Selected option | 4 | 11 | 8 | 25 | 41 |
| *Special "1½" retirement* | | | | | |
| Eligible | — | 96 | 72 | 19 | 149 |
| Selected option | — | 46 | 54 | 17 | 51 |
| TOTAL | | | | | |
| Eligible | 46 | 210 | 192 | 61 | 307 |
| Selected option | 9 | 84 | 110 | 58 | 190 |
| Percentage of workers accepting out of total eligible | 20 | 40 | 57 | 95 | 62 |
| Percentage of workers accepting out of total covered by agreement | 2 | 9 | 10 | 7 | 19 |

pact of pensions in the two cases. In addition, despite the modest numbers involved, it is significant that in Oklahoma City, Fort Worth, and the second Kansas City shutdown there were more pensioners than interplant transferees.

Second, there was wide variation in the proportion of eligible workers who ultimately selected a retirement option. The ratio of selection to eligibility ranged from 20 per cent in Oklahoma City to 95 per cent in the first Kansas City layoff. With the exception of Kansas City, the greatest gap between eligibility and selection was found among those who qualified for early retirement. For them, the reduction in benefits associated with early retirement (6 per cent for each calendar year under 65 years of age) was sufficient to make the other options relatively more attractive.

During the interviews prior to displacement, it was commonplace to see individual workers struggling to compare the financial advantages of pension payments of unknown duration with the certain benefits to be derived from severance pay. In fact, most of those workers who changed their decisions chose to receive a lump sum separation payment instead.

As seen in Table 7, the Kansas City experience with the acceptance of pension benefits was sharply differentiated from that of the previous shutdowns. Here, a high proportion of the eligible workers selected early retirement in comparison with the record in other cities, while a relatively low proportion of workers chose the special "1½" pension. The reasons for the greater attraction of early retirement for the displaced workers in Kansas City can only be conjectured.

In January, 1965, the pension formula was increased from $2.50 to $3.25 per month for each year of service. This meant that those who were eligible for early retirement as a result of the second layoff in Kansas City received greater benefits than the workers who were displaced from the other plants. Conceivably, the increase in absolute benefit levels was now sufficient to persuade many workers to accept a pension even though the early retirement formula involved a percentage reduction in the amount to which they were entitled. On the other hand, the limited resort to the special "1½" pension in Kansas City may be attributed to the fact that many transfer opportunities existed in Armour plants in the same general area. Under the circumstances, the employee who was between 55 and 60 years of age could choose to exercise his rights under the interplant transfer program and to continue working until normal retirement age, if possible. In any case, the Kansas City experience vividly reveals the perils of developing an adjustment program on fixed expectations concerning the response of displaced workers to a set of options in a particular situation.

Of the three pension options, early retirement and the special "1½" pension had the greatest relevance to the displaced employees. They offered alternatives to workers who normally would have the dimmest prospects of finding satisfactory full-time jobs in the labor market at large. Nevertheless, the decision to accept a pension was not an easy or complete solution to the financial problems arising from displacement. Even the most generous alternative was associated with a drastic reduction in income. A 65-year-old worker with thirty years of service who retired with full pension received $75 per month before January 1, 1965. After that date, he would receive $97.50 per month. The same amounts would be paid to an employee who met the minimum, but substantial, eligibility requirements for the special "1½" retirement option. It is clear that in most cases supplementary funds would have to be forthcoming from such other sources as savings, Social Security, or employment of some sort to meet current living expenses. Few private plans today are designed to satisfy the full monetary needs of the pensioner. The Armour experience indicates however, that for many workers some form of retirement income will constitute the preferred method of reducing the economic impact of permanent displacement.

## The Role of Financial Cushions

Severance pay and pension plans have been important elements in the company and unions' program to deal with the consequences of large-scale labor displacement. For many workers, they offer the bird-in-the-hand that is preferable to the uncertainties and the personal costs of interplant transfer. By itself, however, severance pay does not seem to have an inordinate influence on the displaced workers' judgment. Rather, the widespread acceptance of severance pay merely highlights the intrinsic or administrative deficiencies of other options. There is little evidence that the separation allowance is dissipated by what might be generally considered frivolous purchases. On the contrary, a major problem in the use of severance pay appears to be the reduction of the net amount available for living expenses after heavy debt obligations have been met. Another, peripheral difficulty has been the short-run effect of the receipt of severance pay on the displaced worker's claim to other forms of transitional income, particularly unemployment compensation.

These problems should not obscure the basic strength and attraction of severance pay as part of a program to cope with the problems of displacement. Where far-reaching changes in plant location and technology are introduced in a relatively short period of time, as in the Armour situation, the main arena of manpower adjustment inevitably will be the labor market at large. Despite its limitations, severance pay provides some assurance that the worker will not enter this arena empty-handed. On the relationship between severance pay and labor market experience, many significant questions still remain unanswered.

The Armour experience also reveals that pension plans can make a significant contribution to the process of adjustment, especially where they are adapted to the special circumstances of a plant shutdown. In this respect, the special "1½" pension recognizes the real distinction between voluntary retirement and the extraordinary occurrences that may make a premature decision to retire advisable. Many workers facing permanent displacement have turned to the various retirement options when they could under the existing eligibility requirements.

Various criticisms may be lodged against both pensions and severance pay. Neither "solves" the problems of large-scale displacement in any real sense. Similarly, both may be criticized on the grounds that they provide inadequate income to satisfy the needs of the unemployed workers. Severance pay may be cynically viewed as "conscience money," and the "early retirement" of those who are willing and able to work can be considered socially wasteful. It should be recalled, however, that as "financial cushions" these measures are never designed to bear the full burdens of displacement. Rather, as the metaphor itself indicates, they were established to mitigate the shock of drastic economic change. This more limited objective also adds to the range of alternatives from which the individual may choose while providing support for subsequent remedial efforts.

# 5 *Placement Campaigns in Labor Markets*

THE labor market inevitably plays a crucial role in the process of manpower adjustment to economic change. This role is dramatically apparent when large-scale displacement takes place within a short period of time, as was true of the Armour shutdowns. Initially, the availability and scope of alternative job opportunities will affect the operation of such internal mechanisms of adjustment as the interplant transfer program. Thus the limited range of employment opportunities available in the Sioux City labor market doubtless stimulated selection of the transfer option. Even when the transfer program involves a substantial number of workers, as it did in Sioux City and Kansas City, it is unlikely that this measure will help a majority of the displaced workers. The process of finding jobs in other companies and industries therefore assumes great importance in any comprehensive effort to deal with labor displacement. With this judgment in mind, the Automation Fund Committee has organized various efforts to help the displaced workers develop, understand, and market their skills.

The strategy of any placement campaign must take into account three main elements: the level and structure of demand for labor; the characteristics and skills of the job seekers; and the nature and organization of the labor market itself. The success of any campaign will then depend upon how favorable each factor is to the goals of the placement effort, and the skill exercised in exploiting the available opportunities. The general level of demand in the relevant labor market is, of course, an overriding consideration. A small private group, however, can do little to influence this variable beyond exerting the political influence at its command to help cultivate national and local policies conducive to the growth of employment opportunities.

97

## The Labor Markets: The Scope of Economic Opportunity

The principal experiences of the committee with placement efforts have been in Oklahoma City, Fort Worth, Sioux City, and Kansas City. The small plant in Birmingham, Alabama was closed at a time when the committee was not operative, and no systematic efforts were made there.

The four labor markets that were the focus of the committee's action varied in size, composition of demand, and in employment trends during the most active phase of the placement effort. The Oklahoma City labor market embraces approximately 150,000 workers. At the time of the Armour shutdown, it had an unemployment rate of slightly over 3 per cent. As the committee's program in that city took shape, the incidence of joblessness rose until, in the winter following the shutdown, the area was classified as one of moderate labor surplus, with an unemployment rate in excess of 5 per cent. The impact of the Armour closing had been magnified by substantial layoffs in a large steel fabricating firm, and by cutbacks in construction and in the oil fields. The decline in construction was particularly significant because this sector might normally provide at least short-term employment for unskilled workers.

Employment in Oklahoma City was concentrated in the distributive trades and government, with a heavy emphasis on white-collar occupations. Only about 12 percent of the labor force worked in manufacturing. Thus, few semiskilled jobs were available in Oklahoma City that might offer comparable remuneration to the former Armour workers. It may be noted finally that Oklahoma City is distant from larger urban concentrations and thus from other important labor markets.

The Fort Worth labor market, in contrast, afforded the committee considerable latitude in administering its program. At the time of the major layoffs from the Armour plant in June, 1962, the labor force in the Fort Worth area totaled 222,000, and it remained at this general level in the succeeding period. Approximately 50,000 people were employed in manufacturing and 160,000 in nonmanufacturing industries. Agriculture comprised only a small fraction of the labor force.

The manufacturing sector was dominated by the large aerospace facility operated by General Dynamics. In recent years, employment at the plant has fluctuated between 11,000 and 18,000. The aircraft industry was also represented by the Bell Helicopter Company, which employed several thousand workers. Although overshadowed by the aircraft firms, substantial manufacturing employment was provided by the food products, machinery, and fabricated metals industries in Fort Worth. Following the shutdown of the Armour plant, over 7,000 workers in the area were still engaged in the food products industry.

Nonmanufacturing employment has shown considerable strength in the local labor market. From 1961 to 1962 the number of jobs in retail trade increased from 41,000 to 47,000 with the opening of several large shopping centers. An additional 14,000 workers were employed in wholesale trade. Other leading nonmanufacturing sectors were service industries, private household work, and the government. Over 24,000 persons were employed by various government agencies.

During the course of the committee's program in Fort Worth, the employment situation became more stable. In June, 1962, the unemployment rate was 5.3 per cent. The labor market picture changed, however, in early 1963. Employment prospects at General Dynamics improved with the award of the TFX contract to that firm. Bell Helicopter added about 900 workers, and two furniture manufacturers also registered a modest increase in employment. As a result of these and other additions to demand, the unemployment rate in Fort Worth declined to about 4.5 per cent, giving a more optimistic quality to the labor market.

In addition, Fort Worth is almost contiguous with Dallas, where the labor force numbered about 525,000 and where the unemployment rate had been close to 3 per cent for some time. There is a traditional antagonism between these two cities; nevertheless, they are only 30 miles apart and are linked by a well-developed network of highways.

Sioux City, Iowa, offered a sharp contrast to the first two cases. The labor force there numbered approximately 40,000. Though the unemployment rate seldom rose above 4 per cent—even after the Armour plant shutdown, which affected 3 per cent of the labor force—the demand for labor was relatively stagnant. Furthermore, the local labor market had barely recovered from the 1954 closing of a Cudahy plant that had employed about 1,600 workers. Sioux City is basically a trading area set in the midst of a large and prosperous agricultural belt. The manufacturing sector numbered only about 7,000 and, as the Cudahy and Armour shutdowns indicate, employment in the previously dominant industry, meatpacking, had contracted sharply. Following the Armour shutdown, Swift and Company laid off 200 workers at the only remaining major packing plant. In this case, the committee operated in a relatively small and self-contained labor market where the over-all employment situation was good, but where the structure of demand was unfavorable to workers with an attachment to manufacturing. In addition, the short-run prospects for an expansion of labor demand were not auspicious.

Kansas City falls into the conventional pattern of a large urban labor market. The total labor force in 1964 consisted of 470,000 workers, of whom about 150,000 were employed in manufacturing, transportation, and public utilities. The manufacturing sector included a wide variety of durable and nondurable goods industries, offering an equally diverse array of job opportunities to the displaced workers. Although the unemployment rate shortly after the shutdown was 4.8 per cent, the amount of joblessness was not increasing. In addition, the announcement that General Motors would build a large new installation in Kansas City promised to increase the demand for labor.

The labor markets in which the committee operated had one thing in common: none of the communities enjoyed boom conditions at or following the time of the shutdowns. Beyond this sobering likeness, however, the various labor markets were quite different in structure and level of demand. These differences, in turn, called for adjustments in the implementation of the various placement programs. In Sioux City, a small community where unemployment was low but demand was stagnant, there was little variety in the jobs available. In Fort Worth, the unemployment rate was considerably higher than in Sioux City; however, the situation improved in the course of the placement program, and the labor market was large and diverse. The Oklahoma City labor market was medium-sized, with a relatively small manufacturing sector, and unemployment rose there during the critical period of the placement program. Kansas City was a broad-based urban labor market with a moderate unemployment rate.

## Characteristics of the Job-Seekers

Though the labor markets varied, there was considerable uniformity in the character of the job-seekers. As already indicated, the labor force in the meatpacking industry consists largely of unskilled and semiskilled workers, and many of the higher skills have little transferability in the labor market at large. For example, a skilled beef-boner could scarcely expect to find a ready market for his occupational aptitudes in the durable goods industries. Even for maintenance workers, problems of transferability arose. Although some craftsmen, such as electricians and maintenance machinists, could readily apply their trades in different industrial situations, millrights, scale repairmen, and railroad car repairmen made up a bundle of skills that in large measure were peculiar to the requirements of the meatpacking industry.

These deficiencies in the industrial transferability of meatpacking skills were aggravated by the demographic characteristics of the job-seekers. In each of the cities involved, the average age of the work force exceeded 45 years. This meant that a substantial proportion of the displaced employees were over 50 and could anticipate great reluctance on the part of other employers to hire them.

The age barriers to employability were reinforced by racial and ethnic factors. In Oklahoma City, over 50 per cent of the displaced workers were Negroes. In Fort Worth, the proportion of Negroes in the labor force was only 35 per cent, but an additional 15 per cent were Latin Americans who faced more subtle but equally effective forms of discrimination in Texas. These handicaps were least common in Sioux City, where the overwhelming majority of the workers were white. However, there were special problems in this city. In addition to the handful of Negroes formerly employed at the Armour plant in Sioux City, there was a sizable group of American Indians, who bore a certain stigma in the community. Moreover, since 1950 the meatpacking industry in Sioux City had attracted many displaced persons from Eastern Europe—people who could function effectively in a technical environment requiring strong hands and backs, but who suffered from language and other cultural deficiencies that would reveal themselves when they sought new employment. In Kansas City, the approximately 75 per cent of the Armour employees who were either Negroes or Latin Americans meant special difficulties for any placement campaign.

The problems associated with occupational background, age, and race were not alleviated by any strength in formal education; Ph.D.'s are seldom found in packing houses. In fact, the average educational level of the displaced workers was substantially below that of the population as a whole. In Oklahoma City, Fort Worth, and Kansas City, the labor force averaged approximately eight years of formal education. A few of the younger workers had progressed as far as college, but these rare cases were heavily overbalanced by employees who might be classed as functionally illiterate. The educational level was somewhat higher in Sioux City, where half the workers had ten or more years of formal schooling. But few of these workers had built on this educational base in the period since they had left the classroom.

By any standard, the job-seekers in Oklahoma City, Fort Worth, Sioux City, and Kansas City suffered evident disadvantages in the labor market. That they were entering that market under conditions inauspicious for ready re-employment was further ground for pessimism. Moreover, the earlier experiences of displaced workers in Columbus, Ohio, in East St. Louis, Illinois, and in Fargo, North Dakota suggested that, without any concerted effort at placement, the jobless among the former Armour workers were likely to range from 30 per cent to as high as 50 per cent. Thus an effective placement program would have to mobilize the resources of both private and public agencies concerned with improving the circumstances of the unemployed.

### Administering the Placement Campaigns

In a placement program two basic functions are involved. First, there must be extensive collection, analysis, and dissemination of information. On the supply side, this means that job-seekers should know something of the nature and number of present openings or prospects in the labor market. On the demand side, employers should be aware of particular skills and attributes among the job-seekers. In the absence of such information, the matching process in labor market operation cannot take place except on a random basis.

Second, there must be action on the basis of the information that has been collected and disseminated. Job-seekers must be encouraged to base their search on the realities of the current labor market. Similarly, the employer must be stimulated to consider hiring the designated applicants. In actual practice, these two functions are often carried out simultaneously. However, the analytical distinction must be kept in mind in determining the best division of functions between a private group, such as the Automation Fund Committee, and other agencies that operate in the same area. Essentially, the committee's role was that of an intermediary whose functions would be adapted to the requirements of the particular labor market situation.

## Getting the Program Under Way

The obvious first step toward establishing a communication link between the job-seekers and the labor market is to set up a focal point for the gathering and dissemination of market data. In each city a full-time office was maintained by the committee on a convenient site known to the displaced workers. These offices were staffed by women drawn from the original plant work force, who were thus known to and accepted by the displaced workers and who, in turn, were familiar with meatpacking jobs and workers. In addition, the committee retained the services of a professional person knowledgeable in the operation of labor markets, who supervised the activities of the office and carried out many of its functions. It may be noted that the persons selected to administer the committee's offices on a full-time basis provided invaluable services and fully capitalized upon their familiarity with the people and the plants.

Once an office was established, attention had to be given to the tedious but essential tasks of record-keeping and housekeeping. Files were set up covering all the displaced workers in the bargaining unit, and included information on personal characteristics, jobs previously held in the company, and other incidental data. For the greater part, this information was obtained from company records. Eventually, the files on individual workers were separated into control groups as the workers took up options in the over-all program, so that administrators could immediately identify those who came within its scope. For example, workers who elected to transfer to other Armour plants were generally excluded from the placement program, whereas those who had enrolled in a full-time retraining course were placed in an "inactive" category until they approached completion of the course.

An important element in launching the placement effort was the repeated announcement among the displaced workers that the committee was in business and might be used by those seeking help. To operate effectively, the committee had to obtain the recognition and support of the clientele it hoped to serve. Once a few displaced workers used the committee's services, it was likely that the grapevine would carry the word to a wider audience.

## Working with Other Intermediaries: The Role of the Employment Service

In view of its own relatively limited resources and the need for quick action, it was imperative for the Automation Fund Committee to utilize the services of other agencies concerned with placing workers in new jobs. Of these, the public employment service office in each of the four cities had the central role. The service's approach and relationship with the committee were different in each city, and these differences undoubtedly affected the results of the campaign. The results were more impressive when the employment service assumed an active role in the campaign and made the Armour workers a focus of attention than when its efforts merely followed established routines. These differences are sharply revealed by a consideration of the activities of the employment service in each of the cities involved.

*Oklahoma City:* The Oklahoma City shutdown, it will be recalled, occurred before a contractual provision for advance notice had been negotiated, and the plant was closed about one month after the announcement. The committee's efforts here were largely improvised, since there was little opportunity for preparation. Nor was the employment service equipped with any special procedures to handle problems of this kind.

The committee representatives initially found that the former Armour workers viewed the employment service primarily as an agency for the distribution of unemployment compensation rather than as a source of assistance in finding a job. To help overcome this attitude, and to gather detailed information about the job-seekers, arrangements were made for the local employment service office to provide testing and counseling services for the displaced Armour employees. The familiar territory of the plant cafeteria was used for this purpose. All of the people on the seniority list were invited to take part in the program, and 143 men, about 41 per cent of the total, and 27 women, or 35 per cent, participated in the job counseling and took the General Aptitude Test Battery.

These measures were viewed as a preliminary step in the placement process; but the results were discouraging. According to Professor Edwin Young, who conducted the project for the committee, "The employment service accepted applications and referred workers when appropriate opportunities arose, but most often it referred the workers directly to the casual labor pool. This is not said in criticism of the employment service. Employers simply were not looking for unskilled, middle-aged workers in what was becoming a surplus labor market. . . . It must be said that nearly all the job opportunities for former Armour employees during 1960 and early 1961 were obtained by the workers themselves."

*Fort Worth:* The circumstances in Fort Worth were more favorable for an active placement campaign than in Oklahoma City. Initially, the 90 days' advance notice gave more time to organize the campaign. Moreover, since the actual shutdown took place gradually over a three-month period, the work force was displaced into the labor market in smaller increments. Accordingly, it was possible for the employment service to take preparatory measures before layoffs occurred and to deal with the job-seekers in more manageable groups. Arrangements were made with the Texas Employment Commission to send staff personnel to the Armour plant to interview and register employees as they were terminated. Unfortunately, this arrangement lasted for only a week; then a shortage of funds, the result of a stalemate on all appropriation bills in Congress, caused the TEC to discharge its temporary personnel and to cut back on special services.

The Texas Employment Commission did continue to maintain separate records dealing with the Armour workers, and close liaison was established by the committee with the local office.

During the five-week period in which the heaviest layoffs occurred, the committee representative drew up a weekly list of the terminated employees, gave them an occupational classification, and forwarded the data to the TEC office. The TEC, in turn, checked the qualifications of the terminated employees against its "demand list" of unfilled employer orders to determine whether the two could be matched. However, because the "demand list" generally was concerned with special skills, only three job opportunities were turned up in this process and no placements were made.

Arrangements were also made with the Dallas office of the Texas Employment Commission to aid in the placement campaign. A special procedure was set up for referring former Armour employees to jobs in the Dallas area. This procedure yielded six known jobs, and helped to stimulate unemployed workers to canvass the Dallas labor market themselves; but it barely made a dent in the over-all problem.

At the committee's request—primarily in connection with the retraining program to be described in the next chapter—the employment service in Fort Worth extended its program to include counseling and testing. Special test sessions were scheduled in the evening to accommodate those who could not come during normal office hours. Ultimately, 250 of the former Armour workers underwent testing and/or counseling.

Aside from these steps undertaken at the request of the committee, the employment service generally limited its activities to routine placement, with no attempt to treat the Armour group as a special case, notwithstanding the obvious problems of these workers as individuals and the special circumstances of the large-scale layoff. Thus, the program implemented by the employment service did use the lead time between the advance notice and the actual shutdown, but it did not capitalize on the opportunity to develop a package of measures to cope with this particular situation.

*Sioux City:* The organization of the employment service's

program—and the extent of its cooperation with the Automation Fund Committee—in Sioux City contrasted sharply with the two earlier experiences. Here, the employment service entered the picture quickly and mobilized professional resources in an imaginative manner to attack the problems at hand. Three days after the announcement of the impending shutdown, a labor market analyst from the state administrative office visited the plant to secure detailed information on the characteristics of the employees. Lengthy interviews with all employees were conducted by a special mobile team of employment service counselors. Reports on 857 people were completed before the plant closed, and 206 were given the General Aptitude Test Battery at the plant. The data collected were recorded on punch cards, and special analyses were made for use by the local office and for distribution to other interested parties. This information provided valuable guides for planning and executing subsequent actions.

As part of its "special project" orientation to the Armour shutdown, the Sioux City employment service designated one individual as a liaison with the committee. The skills and potentialities of the displaced group were widely publicized in the local labor market and over a radius of 200 miles. Special efforts were made to contact other employers in the meatpacking industry. On a local radio station a daily program, "Armour Ringing," was set up to issue brief reports on the capabilities of selected jobseekers. The employment service also helped stimulate the formation of a Citizens Re-employment Committee, with representation from all segments of the community, to help promote jobs for the displaced workers. Meanwhile, the counseling and testing were continued; nine months after the plant closing, 461 of the displaced workers had been given the GATB.

The initiative developed by the employment service before and immediately following the shutdown was sustained in succeeding periods. In the spring of 1964, nine months after the shutdown, another placement campaign was launched for those still unemployed. For this effort, worker and employer lists were carefully matched. Meanwhile, supplementary steps were taken to exploit the national network for job clearance developed by the employment service so that Sioux City workers could actively consider jobs that were available in other cities in Iowa and throughout the Midwest.

*Kansas City:* In Kansas City, the pattern developed in the Sioux City case was further amplified. Because agencies of two states were involved, planning began at the federal and regional levels of the Bureau of Employment Security. (Kansas City, Missouri and Kansas City, Kansas are contiguous communities and are regarded as a single, comprehensive labor market. Although the Armour plant was located in Missouri, many of the workers lived on the Kansas side. In addition, the quest for job opportunities would clearly overlap those segments of the market that were in both states.) There were meetings in Washington, D.C., of representatives of the Automation Fund Committee and the United States Employment Service. Once this groundwork had been laid, the site of administrative action was quickly moved to Kansas City. Testing and interviewing were begun before the shutdown; special liaison officers were appointed in local offices of the employment service; and a concerted effort was made to analyze the characteristics of the displaced workers in the light of available employment opportunities. Clearly, both the Automation Fund Committee and the employment service had profited from their earlier experiences.

In any moderate-sized or large labor market, intermediaries other than the public employment service will be present and may be utilized in carrying out a general placement campaign. The help they provide, however, will probably be limited. Private intermediaries fall into two general categories: nonprofit agencies with a social service orientation, which concentrate on aiding individuals with special disabilities; and private fee-charging agencies, which attempt to serve broad segments of the labor market. Agencies of the former type, such as Goodwill Industries, can be useful in dealing with unique cases. In Fort Worth, for example, Goodwill Industries expended considerable effort in attempting to find a job for a worker with an amputated leg who had been "carried" in an easy job in the meatpacking plant following the loss of the limb. Similarly, church groups provided some job leads in Fort Worth and Sioux City.

Fee-charging employment agencies, on the other hand, were contacted but never used. The better jobs offered by these agencies generally involved special skills that were in short supply in the labor market. Workers who possessed such skills believed, usually correctly, that they could find jobs on their own initiative. Workers without distinguishing occupational qualifications were reluctant to "buy" a job that paid low wages and had limited long-run prospects. In the absence of help from the public employment service or the committee, displaced workers were most likely to fall back on informal sources of information, such as friends and relatives.

### The Role of the Automation Fund Committee

The role and functions of the Automation Fund Committee in the administration of the placement campaigns were determined in a large degree by the scope of the employment service's activities. While the committee was constantly aware that it "represented" the former Armour workers in their dealings with the public agency, its direct involvement in the placement process varied from case to case.

In Oklahoma City and Fort Worth, the relatively routine efforts of the employment service were supplemented with an intensive program carried out by the committee. The Oklahoma City project is summarized in a Progress Report of the committee:

Careful lists of former Armour employees and their qualifications were drawn and made available to interested employers; personal calls were made on company representatives to acquaint them with former Armour personnel and to attempt to persuade them to hire such persons. Newspaper, radio, and television publicity were sought and exploited. All of this supplemented contacts already made through the Armour employment office with other employers, particularly in the meatpacking industry.

As employment conditions worsened, however, these efforts were not productive of any direct placement. As Professor Young later summarized, "While the staff of the Automation Committee looked for jobs, it found very few, perhaps making its greatest contribution by developing in the prospective employers an interest in the former Armour workers."

In Fort Worth the committee further expanded the range of its placement activities. Personal visits were made to thirty employers in the surrounding area, with the active cooperation of the Chamber of Commerce. The firms were selected to meet several criteria: they were usually the larger employers; their occupational mix included a substantial number of unskilled or semiskilled workers; they were known to be expanding their operations; or they used workers in occupational categories roughly comparable to those found in the meatpacking industry. Discussions were held with the chief executive of the firm or establishment, followed by a meeting with the personnel manager. The purpose and program of the Automation Fund Committee were described in detail, and the cooperation of the company was solicited in making known any present or future job opportunities. To this end, the personnel manager was given an occupational breakdown of Armour employees available for work and the telephone number of the committee's office. Company officials were also asked about occupational skills in short supply in the firm's recent experience, thus providing information that could be useful in the committee's retraining activities.

The response to these visits ranged from cordiality to outright hostility. From discussions with this sampling of local employers it was apparent that there were several major obstacles to the reemployment of these displaced workers. It may be noted that these same considerations were operative in Oklahoma City, and to a lesser extent, in Sioux City:

1. Identification of these workers with a union with a reputation for militancy. Without exception, every nonunion employer stated directly or by inference that he would be reluctant to hire a former Armour workers because of their union background. Moreover, a few nonunion employers stated that all applicants must take a "TVT." (Truth Verification or Lie Detector Test) as part of an exploration of crucial elements in their employment history and personal background. The jobs involved were relatively unskilled and poorly paid, and the employers appeared anxious to screen out applicants with strong union sympathies.

2. The relatively high wage experience of the displaced workers. Many employers stated that former Armour workers were accustomed to wages substantially higher than those that prevailed in the community for semiskilled work, that they feared these people would be dissatisfied with the lower wage offered, and that this dissatisfaction would spread to others in the plant. These fears, of course, were related to concern over unionization and its potential effects. One furniture manufacturer flatly declared: "We are a low wage firm and we intend to keep it that way."

3. Discrimination against racial and ethnic groups. As noted earlier, about half the labor force involved was composed of Negroes and Latin Americans. At the time Fort Worth had a tight pattern of segregation in education and in accepted designations of what kinds of jobs would be open to various categories of persons. As might be expected, the opportunities for Negroes and Latins generally were limited to service and unskilled occupations. Some progress had been made in breaking down these barriers in nearby Dallas, but few changes had taken place in Fort Worth at the time of the shutdown.

One example may illustrate the pattern of distribution of economic opportunity in Fort Worth. In the automobile service department of a large department store Negroes were hired as tire changers, Latin Americans to change batteries, and whites (or "Anglos") to work as station attendants.

4. The age of the displaced workers. The average age of the people involved was approximately 46, and only eight were less than 30 years of age. Many firms had implicit or explicit rules restricting new hires to people under 45 or 40 years of age. In one case, a central

agency placing service station attendants in the Fort Worth area did not accept people over 35 years old.

These efforts to develop job openings through personal visits to a relatively small number of firms were augmented by other measures designed to gather and disseminate labor market information. Letters were sent to about six hundred firms in the Fort Worth area, including all those who employed fifty or more workers, explaining the committee's program and asking their cooperation in helping the displaced workers to find jobs. The letter was signed by the manager of Armour's Fort Worth plant. Cooperation was also obtained from the local electric utility service, which furnished the committee with detailed records on the use of electric power by industrial firms. From these records it was possible to determine which firms were expanding operations. This information was then disseminated to persons who called for job information or who came into the committee's office for one reason or another. In addition, general publicity about the committee's program was obtained through stories in the local newspapers and in appearances before meetings of the Chamber of Commerce and other fraternal groups. This publicity informed the community and also corrected certain erroneous and possibly damaging rumors about the placement program.

One more aspect of the placement program is of practical as well as academic interest, even though the results were disappointing. As everyone who has studied the operation of labor markets knows, the majority of jobs are found as a result of information from friends and relatives on an informal basis. With this in mind, the committee made an effort to formalize the "grapevine" that was presumed to develop among job-seekers. It was supposed that many former Armour employees would be actively canvassing the market and might provide leads for opportunities that, for some reason, they could not or would not accept themselves, but which other employees might accept if they were aware of them.

Several approaches were used in trying to tap this source of information. The committee representative first explored with officers of the local union the feasibility of a system whereby the shop stewards would periodically contact individual members to learn of any job leads. This approach was deemed unworkable because the sharp drop in union membership had produced great instability in the local. In a second attempt, the committee sent a circular to all Armour employees, discussing the importance of disseminating labor market information among themselves and containing a return postcard with appropriate headings on the back. The employees were asked to fill out the postcard and return it to the committee if they heard about particular jobs which, for some reason, they did not want themselves. This turned out to be a monumental failure; only one card was received out of the 970 that had been distributed.

Third, an *ad hoc* approach was used. Former employees who came to the committee office for any reason were asked if they knew of any opportunities. In addition, those who had indicated in a preliminary mail questionnaire that they were currently employed were called by telephone to learn whether they knew of any other vacancies. This method, although more laborious, turned out to be reasonably fruitful. About forty leads were discovered in this manner.

Even though the committee's efforts to organize the "grapevine" were not successful, informal channels of communication apparently did provide the most fruitful source of job leads for the workers. A survey of a random sample of former Armour workers who did not take retraining or otherwise come within the committee's formal program indicated that 85 per cent of the successful job-seekers had found employment through direct application or leads provided by friends and relatives.

The independent activities of the committee in Sioux City and Kansas City, in contrast to those taken in Oklahoma City and Fort Worth, were negligible. In the former, the employment service had organized itself on a special-project basis and had assumed the tasks of contacting employers, obtaining publicity, and analyzing labor market conditions—tasks that the committee had carried out in the other cities. The committee's efforts in Sioux City and Kansas City were aimed at reinforcing and complementing the central programs of the employment service. Thus committee representatives furnished liaison between the employment services and the displaced workers, helping to stimulate use of the employment service by the workers and to increase their understanding of its procedures and objectives. The committee also took a hand in the planning of various specialized placement efforts. In part, this was a matter of giving special help to workers with peculiar handicaps; now and then it was a matter of program development. For example, the procedures for interoffice clearance of job openings utilized in Sioux City were set in motion at the request of the committee. A few plant visits to large employers were made jointly with the local manager of the employment service, who was personally acquainted with the employers and who felt that some face-to-face explanation by a committee representative would be helpful. These efforts of the committee no doubt were helpful to the employment service, but they were essentially supportive and supplementary. The major administrative burdens were handled by the employment service, which with experience had learned to adapt its placement procedures to the special problems posed by plant shutdowns.

## Working with the Individual

In a final aspect of the committee's activities, dealing directly with the displaced workers, its representatives carried out a variety of functions. Counseling was provided to help the workers understand their occupational potentialities. Steps taken to stimulate the process of search for employment in the labor market included discussions of possible opportunities in other labor markets, so that relocation might be viewed as one feasible alternative. And committee representatives tried to foster realistic expectations concerning the labor market. Such direct dealings were mainly with workers who undertook retraining programs. In most cases, an interest in retraining brought the displaced workers into close contact with the committee's representatives.

The adjustment of expectations to the realities of the labor market largely came about with the passage of time and with the post-shutdown experiences of the job-seekers. Discussions with committee and employment service counselors, however, provided the job-seekers with a broader range of information against which to evaluate their own experiences. This information generally confirmed the fact that lower wages were to be expected where opportunities were available. The discussions helped a worker to decide whether any given job offer was in line with other possible opportunities, although the wages might be substantially below the income they received on their previous jobs with Armour.

The problem of adjusting expectations is illustrated in an incident reported by the employment service in Sioux City. About three weeks after the shutdown, the service tried to fill an order for a city bus driver. The job paid a starting wage of $1.88 per hour, a good one by local standards but about 60¢ per hour lower, on the average, than the wages paid by Armour. Eleven of the displaced workers, all of whom met the age and other requirements for the job, refused referral, and two others failed to return a completed application to the company. Six months later this job would have been quickly taken. In this case, the counseling had not yet been given a sense of reality by direct experience in the labor market. In general, however, comparative experience suggests that in smaller labor markets, such as that in Sioux City, expectations changed more rapidly than in the larger and more diverse Fort Worth market.

In some cases, a worker's expectations may be affected by the manner in which the process of displacement is administered. That is, a common initial response by displaced workers to permanent layoff is the belief, however illusory, that the situation is not irrevocable and that rehirings are imminent. Usually, this belief is based on groundless rumors. However, if the layoff procedure is carried out in a manner that gives credence to the rumors, it becomes difficult to orient the displaced workers to a realistic appraisal of their chances in the labor market. Thus, the Kansas City shutdown involved several major departments rather than the complete Armour facility. As the company adjusted its manpower requirements to the new technical circumstances, it became necessary to recall some workers who had been "permanently" displaced. The recalls immediately gave rise to similar expectations on the part of other displaced workers. During this period, it was extremely difficult to persuade these workers to accept any of several attractive job opportunities offered through the employment service.

Counseling was also important in rediscovering the latent skills of the individual by helping him to explore and evaluate his work experience outside the packing house. New light might be shed on the individual's occupational prospects by discussing his military service, his job history, any special training that he might have undertaken, and the skills developed through hobbies or other leisure-time activities. A large variety of capabilities were identified by this process. In some cases, the individual was advised to take a short retraining course in order to restore an old skill and make it marketable. The possibilities open to such occupational flexibility are virtually unlimited:

One worker in Fort Worth had had experience in the operation of a launderette which gave him some knowledge of appliance repair. He was able to obtain a job as an appliance repairman for a local department store.

A "leg puller" in the Sioux City plant had previous experience in the excavation operations of construction projects. He was placed by the employment service as a dragline operator at a wage of $2.50 per hour.

A stock clerk had been employed as a machinist in the aircraft industry. After a short retraining course, he was placed as a lathe operator in a small metal-working plant.

A woman whose hobby was photography set up a business as a dog photographer after building up her skills to a professional level.

The assessment of the individual's occupational flexibility may not be sufficient to stimulate effective labor market behavior. In many cases, it may be necessary to help him develop the motivation and ability to conduct a continued and intelligent pattern of search. Frequently, after an initial random foray into the labor market had been unsuccessful, the job-seeker gave up in despair or frustration. Because many workers had not sought new employment for as much as two decades, they could profit from guidance on how to go about canvassing the labor market.

As a first step, job leads were provided. Since many of the people were functionally illiterate or literate only in Spanish, want ads in the local paper were read and discussed with them. Sometimes it was necessary to help the employee fill out an application form. In other instances, the individual had little appreciation of how physical appearance could influence the outcome of a job interview. Here, simple suggestions on personal grooming could be helpful.

The results of these highly personalized services were often indirect. A specific lead or suggestion might be fruitless, but the process of search initiated by the suggestion might turn up other opportunities and, ultimately, a job. For example, a former employee in Fort Worth was given an introduction slip to the Dallas office of the Texas Employment Service. While driving to Dallas, he stopped at a suburban industrial center and inquired about employment. As a result, he was hired by one of the firms at the center.

Another effort to promote search in local labor markets consisted of suggestions by the committee intended to broaden the geographical scope of job-seeking. This approach was particularly important in Sioux City because of the limited dimensions of that labor market. The response was limited, but a small group of people were willing to follow up the suggestion. However, much of this movement was aimless and lacked any specific orientation. The job clearance procedures developed by the employment service can be useful in these cases, but typically are unknown to job-seekers.

Although some people are willing to move geographically, the barriers to movement are real and can frustrate what otherwise appear to be encouraging prospects. Efforts by the committee to interest Fort Worth employees in jobs located in the Dallas area met with success in only a handful of cases despite the proximity of this large and booming labor market. The reputation of Dallas as a "low wage" town, the irrational but intense rivalry between Fort Worth and Dallas, and the costs of transportation or moving, modest though they might be, apparently weighed heavily as factors restricting interest in these job opportunities.

## The Campaign Results

The results of the placement campaigns are difficult to measure with precision. In many cases, those provided with job leads did not call back to report the outcome of their applications. Moreover, it is virtually impossible to give any quantitative weight to such measures as visits to prospective employers, the intensive counseling of job-seekers, and other indirect elements of the placement campaigns. These difficulties are compounded in an effort at comparative evaluation of the different campaigns. Differences in the structure of the labor market, the characteristics of the job-seekers, and the short-run demand for labor all limit the bases for objective comparison. Nonetheless, in context, the available data can shed some light on the efficacy of the placement activities in the various cities. Perhaps the most vivid results are those concerning the employment service. No systematic totals were kept by its local offices in Oklahoma City or Fort Worth, but in both the record of direct placement appears to be negligible. In Oklahoma City, only a handful of former Armour workers were known to have found jobs through the employment service in the first year after the shutdown. The results in Fort Worth were equally limited. Interviews with a random sample of 180 displaced Armour workers revealed that only 3.5 per cent of those who were employed attributed their jobs to leads provided by the employment service. When this percentage is applied to the total population from which the sample was drawn, a total of approximately fourteen placements can be credited to the employment service.[1]

Even allowing for possible deficiencies in the data, the success of the employment service in finding new opportunities for displaced Armour workers in Sioux City stands in sharp contrast to the record compiled in Oklahoma City and Fort Worth. In the twenty-three months following the plant shutdown, the Sioux City office of the Iowa Employment Service, which maintained special files for the project, placed 422 former Armour workers in other jobs in the local labor market.[2] This achievement becomes more impressive when account is taken of the narrow range of job opportunities in Sioux City. Clearly, the broad-based campaign launched by the employment service had tangible and constructive results. Although the program in Kansas City was still in its formative stages in the spring of 1964, the use of a similar "special project" approach to the placement effort was the basis for some optimism.

The outcome of the supplementary placement activities carried out by the Automation Fund Committee in Oklahoma City and

---

[1] The total population comprised 550 displaced workers who were not retired, had not transferred, and were not enrolled in retraining courses. The survey revealed that approximately 70 per cent of those interviewed were working. Also, it is known from Automation Fund Committee records that none of the retrainees obtained jobs through the employment service.

[2] It should be noted that an undetermined number of these 422 placements were seasonal, associated with the pre-Christmas or spring increases in business. Also, an undetermined number of placements represent second placements of persons who were laid off after initial placement and were re-employed later in other vacancies developed by the service. Nonetheless, in comparison with the Oklahoma City and Fort Worth experiences, where the same considerations applied, the results of the Sioux City campaign were prodigious.

Fort Worth provided evidence of the limited potentialities of a temporary, private agency in this area. No direct placements at all were made by the committee in Oklahoma City. It should be recalled, however, that the committee's placement program in that city was restricted to visits to potential employers, and that no attempt was made to serve as an active intermediary in the labor market. On the other hand, the committee avowedly assumed the role of a placement agency in Fort Worth. Its efforts led to approximately 400 job referrals of one kind or another, resulting in forty-six known placements. While some comfort may be derived from the observation that the number of placements made by the committee was three times as many as the estimated total for the employment service, this record was hardly encouraging. It was these results that caused the committee to adjust its strategy and to press for the more active involvement of the employment service. The Sioux City experience gives some credence to the wisdom of this decision.

Wages constitute another yardstick by which the effectiveness of a placement campaign may be measured. Here the information available permits an unambiguous conclusion—that in each of the three cities the wages earned by those who found jobs as a result of the placement campaign were substantially below the previous levels attained at Armour. In Fort Worth, the wages received on jobs found by the committee and the employment service ranged from $1.15 to $2.00 per hour, as compared to an average wage of approximately $2.65 per hour that prevailed at Armour. In Sioux City, about 90 per cent of those placed received less than the Armour average. Clearly, job placement did not mean maintenance of income. On the other hand, the reduced wages were more desirable than the prospect of prolonged unemployment.

Further perspective on these placement efforts may be obtained by a reference to the aggregate employment experience of male displaced workers.[3] About one year after the plant shutdowns,

---

[3] In each city sample surveys were made of the labor market experience of the displaced workers. The figures for male workers are more significant be-

the employment rate among workers who had not taken retraining and who were actively seeking jobs was 60 per cent in Oklahoma City, 72 per cent in Fort Worth, and 75 per cent in Sioux City. Although substantial unemployment still existed in each city, many individuals had obviously found new niches in the labor market through their own efforts.

## Some Lessons from the Placement Campaign

The differences and similarities, the achievements and the disappointments in these four placement efforts suggest some lessons which may be useful in dealing with similar problems. It has been said again and again that the general level of demand in any labor market will be a major determinant of the success of any placement effort, no matter how energetically pursued. The Automation Fund Committee's experience underlines the accuracy of this statement. Even meatpackers cannot make a silk purse of a sow's ear. At the same time, in all but the most dismal situations, some salutary steps can be taken for a particular group of workers within the latitude afforded by the labor market.

The record compiled by the committee in these four labor markets strongly suggests that best results will be obtained by closely cooperative work with the employment service. Obviously, if the employment service will not invest major resources in the job, a private group will have to shift for itself. However, the results of the extensive efforts by the committee in Oklahoma City and Fort Worth to develop a direct placement program do not permit great optimism for the prospects for this approach. A temporary agency, without deep roots in the community, cannot by itself mount a comprehensive and enduring campaign. On the other hand, blind reliance on the employment service is no assur-

---

cause the labor market participation of women is highly variable. The data for Oklahoma City were collected eight months after the shutdown. In Fort Worth and Sioux City surveys were taken one calendar year after the plant closing.

ance of success either, unless special measures are initiated to meet the problems involved. Unfortunately, business as usual means unemployment as usual. The broad campaign of the employment service in Sioux City, and more recently in Kansas City, indicates what can be done by an energetic group working on a special project basis, focusing available resources on a crucial community problem. If the employment service can develop this pattern widely, it can measure up to its important role in an economy marked by rapidly changing labor conditions.

When the employment service operates at a high level of competence, the role of a private group is best defined as a supplementary one. It can help in the planning by drawing on its unique knowledge of the workers involved and of the shutdown situation; and it can carry out special tasks that for one reason or another are difficult for a public, community-based organization to assume. In addition, a private group can build up the status of the employment service in the eyes of the displaced workers so that they are encouraged to turn to the service as something more than an "unemployment office" for passing on the legitimacy of benefit claims.

If the results of the various placement campaigns indicate that even at its most successful it will only help a minority of the workers, it may be asked, Why are such programs necessary? Since most workers find new employment through their own resources, what is there to justify the formal placement activities of public or private agencies?

First, even though the number of direct placements may be small, an organized placement effort can help create a "sense of mobility" in the labor market on the part of the displaced worker. Through effective counseling he can realistically assess his capabilities, discarding illusions about his prospects and rediscovering marketable skills. And in pursuing leads provided by the placement agency, he is stimulated to carry on the search that is essential to finding new employment.

Second, a formal placement program can offer direct aid to the "difficult cases"—the workers with special disabilities. In fact, many of the placements made in Fort Worth fell into this category. Thus, the incremental contribution of the program will be greater than a simple count of placements implies. In this sense, it becomes one more tool in an array of measures designed to promote worker adjustment.

Third, it follows that an organized placement campaign can also contribute to the effectiveness of the over-all program established by public and private agencies. The decision to transfer or not will be determined in part by available information concerning job opportunities in the local labor market. In addition, retraining is best viewed as part of the placement process. When the trainee completes his course, he will usually have to venture into an unfamiliar sector of the labor market where specialized information is required. As a back-up resource, then, the contribution of the placement effort must be computed on broader terms than direct placements.

Perhaps the outstanding lesson to be derived from these experiences, as related to both public and private efforts, is the necessity for gearing a general campaign to the specialized problems which confront the program administrators. In talking about unemployment, economists customarily generalize; in dealing with the unemployed worker, the labor market administrator must particularize. The campaign is made up of bits and pieces, no one of which may be decisive or broadly significant, but which together can offer substantial aid to job-seekers.

# 6        Experiments with Retraining

ONCE the Automation Fund Committee had decided to extend its efforts to the labor market beyond the firm, occupational retraining was regarded as a logical method for helping the displaced workers to find new employment. The concept of retraining unemployed workers for new occupations has won wide acceptance in the United States and is now embodied in legislation enacted at both the federal and state levels. When the committee took its first steps in this direction, however, only limited experience was available as a guide to action. Consequently the committee initially established a small, experimental program in Oklahoma City. In Fort Worth, Sioux City, and Kansas City the scope of its retraining activities was expanded. Programs in each of these cities drew upon the preceding effort, and together they offer significant insights into the feasibility and the problems of retraining the unemployed.

The rationale for occupational retraining as a cure for unemployment is the assumption that while some workers with minimal or obsolete skills are in a state of involuntary idleness, unfilled jobs are available because of the lack of qualified persons. Obviously, both society and the individual will benefit from an investment intended to equip unemployed workers with the skills appropriate to the available job opportunities. These simple assumptions are far removed, however, from the subtleties of giving them practical application. Retraining may be little more than an extension of the placement effort, giving the unemployed worker a rudimentary grasp of the skills necessary to obtain a new orientation in the labor market and giving potential employers evidence of the worker's seriousness of purpose. Or it may involve an ambitious program to upgrade the occupational proficiencies of the unemployed. And in many situations, the basic concept of "retraining" must be expanded to cover instruction in the basic tools of literacy.

Recognition of this variability in the nature of a retraining program points the way to a possible solution of a basic dilemma that confronts the administrator. The Armour experiences clearly indicate that the persons with the least capacity to absorb training—as measured by education, age, and performance on aptitude tests—are also those most in need of help from some outside agency. On the other hand, the inevitable limitation on resources available to support a retraining program implies that the highest priority should be given to those applicants with the best prospects of success. One way out of this dilemma is to structure the program by varying the scope and labor market orientation of the different retraining options, so that the widest possible range of workers can be served. This approach means, in turn, that heavy burdens are shifted to the program administrators. Indeed, one of the major lessons of the committee's activities is that the theoretical benefits of retraining the unemployed can be derived only from the administrative standards and techniques by which a given program is implemented.

## The Scope of Retraining

The starting point of any retraining program must be a set of policy decisions concerning the selection of the retrainees, the identification of the appropriate occupational categories, and the assignment of individuals to particular retraining courses. There was much variation in the policies adopted for the three major retraining efforts undertaken by the committee, reflecting both different circumstances and basic changes of concept as dictated by experience.[1]

---

[1] Because the retraining program in Kansas City was still in its formative stages in early 1965, it is omitted from the following discussion.

## Oklahoma City

The retraining effort in Oklahoma City was the first experimental measure taken by the Automation Fund Committee to facilitate the adjustment of displaced workers in the labor market. Since the interplant transfer plan had not yet been developed, the committee's efforts were oriented primarily to the labor market at large rather than to the redistribution of economic opportunities within a firm. Consequently, the program was designed to retrain workers for new jobs outside both the firm and the traditional jurisdiction of the UPWA.

As a first step, it will be recalled, the Automation Fund Committee asked the local office of the employment service to conduct counseling interviews and administer the General Aptitude Test Battery (GATB) to all interested workers. One hundred and seventy persons took advantage of this opportunity, including 143 men and 27 women. At this stage of the program, the information obtained from the testing and counseling could be used in connection with the direct placement campaign and also with any retraining effort underwritten by the committee.

When the initial processing was completed, the committee asked the employment service to select those persons who appeared to be best suited for occupational training. The local office counselors chose sixty out of the 170 displaced Armour workers who had been tested. Those excluded by the employment service were not "untrainable" in any profound or absolute sense; but both the Automation Fund Committee and the employment service were venturing into an area in which "standards" were imprecise and often misleading. The selection process has been described by Professor Edwin Young, who was director of the committee's project in Oklahoma City:

It was not implied by the Oklahoma Employment Service that these were the only workers who might be benefited [as a result of retraining]. The selection represented the best judgment of the counselors who, while trained to judge interests and aptitude, had had little or no experience in selecting persons for the kind of experiment undertaken here . . . Most of the workers who had already found jobs as well as a disproportionate share of the younger ones did not take the manual dexterity and general aptitude tests.

Three months after the plant was closed, the basic preparation for the retraining program had been completed. Letters were sent to selected workers informing them of the opportunity to enter a retraining course under the committee's auspices. In addition, all the former Armour employees were notified that they could arrange further testing and counseling by the employment service if they were interested.

Ultimately, fifty-two persons were enrolled in a variety of training courses. Compared with the plant work force as a whole, the trainees had a higher proportion of women, and were slightly younger and better educated; 40 per cent of the trainees were women, the average age was 45, and the median education level was ninth grade. The median seniority was just under twenty years.

Once the retrainees were selected, some standards had to be formulated to guide the approval of specific courses. The committee established three criteria: (1) There was a strong likelihood of employment in the occupation for which the person was being trained. (2) The retrainee had demonstrated aptitude and interest in the occupational area selected. (3) The duration of the training program, and therefore the investment by the committee, would be related consciously to the age of the employee and the type of employment he might obtain as a result of the training. Thus, the committee sought relatively short courses for which the probability of completion would be high and the employment outlook reasonably good.

This approach permitted the selection of a wide array of courses. The fifty-two retrainees received instruction in thirteen different subjects. They included typing, business English, filing and office practice, blueprint reading, welding, basic electronics and electronic mathematics, beautician training, real estate business methods, air conditioning, and auto mechanics. In addition, special classes were arranged for thirteen workers in meat cutting and for fifteen in upholstery.

The Oklahoma City project as a whole was limited in scope and numbers. As a first step, it was designed to test the feasibility of helping selected displaced workers by a program of formal occupational retraining. Authority for the selection of retrainees was delegated to a public agency familiar with counseling and testing techniques, although the project was privately financed. The training courses themselves covered broad sectors of the labor market. Both the private and public agencies were frankly feeling their way.

## Fort Worth

Drawing on the Oklahoma City experience, the Automation Fund Committee established more ambitious goals following the shutdown of the Fort Worth plant. The project to aid the displaced workers had been started before the major layoffs occurred. Thus it was possible to plan in greater detail, and to communicate the details to the individual workers. At the same time, it was hoped that the displaced Armour employees could benefit from the recently passed Manpower Development and Training Act. Substantial effort was expended by the committee to activate the federal program in Fort Worth. By mid-July, however, layoffs were occurring in great numbers, and it became apparent that there would be considerable delay in establishing a federal project to aid Armour workers. In fact, the first MDTA course did not get under way in Fort Worth until January, 1963. In view of the expected delay, it was decided to go ahead with plans for offering retraining under the auspices of the committee.

Steps were taken to inform the workers of the committee's project and to match prospective retrainees with the appropriate training course. First, all employees on the seniority list were notified three times by letter of the opportunity for retraining. These letters outlined the procedure involved. In addition, a meeting was held at the union hall to discuss the committee's program in general and the retraining phase in particular. The meeting was held in two sections—one in the afternoon for workers on the night shift, another in the evening for all other employees. The meetings were attended by 190 people, of whom 128 indicated an immediate interest in retraining.

To help determine his aptitudes, the General Aptitude Test Battery (GATB) was administered to each applicant. Because many of the displaced workers were unfamiliar with such tests, a "preview" instructional session was scheduled. A copy of the GATB was obtained from the employment service, and a test administrator was on hand along with representatives of the company, the union, and the committee. Each category of questions was explained, and efforts were made to reassure the people that no one "passed" or "failed" the test; rather, its purpose was to help determine the occupations for which they might be successfully retrained. The "preview" session was attended by 141 people, including 26 women and 115 men.

The Armour employees took the GATB on a special group basis at the employment service office in Fort Worth. Some night sessions were scheduled to accommodate those who, for various reasons, could not come to the employment service office during the day. The bulk of the testing was completed in two weeks, although stragglers continued to come in over a longer period. Altogether 244 people took the GATB. Following the scoring of the test, each person was asked to participate in a counseling session with a member of the employment service staff. At this session the counselor discussed the general results of the test and explained the individual's "occupational aptitude pattern."

Once the testing and counseling were completed, each person seeking retraining was interviewed by the committee representative to decide on a particular training course. To aid in making these decisions, the committee representative had for each individual, the company personnel card, the GATB score and interpretation; the record of prior education, special training, and work experience; and an interest check list. The counselor's report and evaluation were also available.

On the other side of the labor market, an informal canvass had been made by the committee to determine those occupations for which a reasonable demand might exist in the immediate future. The canvass included conversations with employment service officials, with placement officers at the local vocational school, and with large employers in the community; want ads in the local newspaper also were examined. Concerning the results of this informal canvass, some comfort later came from a more systematic survey completed by the employment service in connection with the federal program. It generally supported the committee's findings.

Certain general policies were established as a guide for handling particular cases. These policies reflected a decision to broaden the program and make it more ambitious. In general, the policies adopted in Fort Worth provided for more generous tuition support and for a wider variety of training programs; and they imposed less stringent standards of acceptability for training. The main policies were as follows:

1. *No applicant was peremptorily denied an opportunity for retraining.* The aim of the interview was to open up vocational opportunities for the individual within the limits of his experience, education, and interests, and the prevailing labor market conditions. Ultimately, a few applicants were not approved for training. These were generally older people with extremely low GATB scores, minimal education, and no well-defined preference for training. In general, the committee set out to help anyone who would try to help himself.

2. *Each applicant was encouraged to conserve or supplement existing skills.* For example, applicants who were already qualified gas or electric welders were advised to take training in heliarc

welding, a skill for which there is a substantial demand in the aerospace industry in the Fort Worth–Dallas area. Similarly, applicants who had prior training in automobile mechanics were advised to take brush-up courses or additional training in motor tune-up techniques. On the other hand, one former Armour employee who was a qualified asbestos coverer was encouraged to canvass the labor market for a job in this trade before enrolling in a training program for a new occupation.

3. *No limitations were imposed on occupational choice, and qualified applicants were not denied training opportunities because of discriminatory standards applied to Negroes and Latin Americans in the local labor markets.* The committee representative would merely comment that the problem existed and that the trainee might face some disappointment unless he or she was willing to go outside the labor market to seek employment. However, the final choice was left to the applicant if he was qualified. The committee was also committed to a strong placement effort in any such case.

4. *Individuals with unusual occupational and training preferences were accommodated insofar as possible even though the labor market survey did not specifically show a need for these occupations.* The theory here was that, in a labor market as broad and diverse as Fort Worth, there would always be room for one more, at the bottom if not at the top. Thus one woman was approved for a course that would qualify her as a piano teacher, although no labor market information was available for this occupation.

Ultimately, 170 persons entered training, including 104 men and 66 women. As at Oklahoma City, the program included a disproportionate number of women; and Negro women, in particular, were heavily represented. The median age of the male trainees was approximately 40, while the women averaged 45 years of age. Half of the group had less than an eighth grade education. This deficiency was further reflected in the GATB scores. The retrainee group as a whole scored considerably less than the median performance of a "normal" population. The Negroes, who had the most limited educational background, generally fell in the lowest 20 per cent. Thus, the Armour retrainees constituted a disadvantaged group by the usual standards, and the Negroes suffered from especially formidable handicaps.

Altogether, the trainees enrolled in thirty-two different courses. The largest enrollments were in auto repair, welding, air conditioning repair and installation, clerical work, food service, retail meatcutting, and warehouse and stock management. The full list of courses is as follows:

General machine repair; auto repair, body and fender; auto repair, automatic transmission; auto repair, engine overhaul; welding, gas and electric; welding, heliarc; air conditioning and refrigeration; refrigeration, truck units; secretarial; accounting; electronics-TV; cashier–checkout clerk; general sales; heavy equipment operator; practical nurse; Diesel mechanic; food service; beauty operator; barber; retail meatcutting; teacher, general education; warehouse and stock management; power sewing machine repair; clothing presser; cooking and baking; real estate agent; floral arrangement; landscaping; animal care; music teaching.

In Fort Worth, then, the program was designed so that retraining was available to virtually everyone who wanted to take advantage of the opportunity. The committee attempted to arrange for each applicant a training course that matched his abilities and held some promise of a payoff in the labor market. In contrast to Oklahoma City, the administrative reins were held more closely by the committee representatives, although the employment service provided important technical help through its counseling and testing programs.

## Sioux City

When the Sioux City shutdown occurred in June, 1963, federally financed training programs authorized by the Manpower Development and Training Act were in operation throughout the country. After the frustrations with MDTA in Fort Worth, this development added a new dimension and supplementary resources to the committee's program of retraining. From the outset, committee representatives worked closely with officials of the Bureau of Employment Security and the Office of Education who were charged with administering the act. The training allowances it provided greatly exceeded anything possible with the committee's resources. Consequently, every effort was made to qualify displaced Sioux City employees for federal programs. Liaison and planning discussions were held with officials at the national, regional, state, and local levels in an effort to establish training programs in good time to meet the individual needs of the Sioux City workers.

Within this expanded framework, the measures taken to initiate the program were essentially the same as those adopted in Fort Worth. Its objectives were explained to the displaced workers in a series of letters and open meetings. A commitment was made to offer a wide variety of retraining options, consistent with available facilities and job prospects for particular occupations in the labor market. The responsibility for initial testing and counseling was again assumed by the local office of the employment service. Because the employment service moved quickly and energetically into the situation within the 90-day advance notice period, it reached a large proportion of the Armour workers. Ultimately, over 800 persons received some counseling, and 480 of these also took the GATB and associated tests as part of the over-all placement and training effort.

Because of the active involvement of various government agencies under MDTA, the role of the committee in Sioux City differed in several respects from that in Fort Worth and Oklahoma City. First, the committee served as a clearing house for information on retraining opportunities developed under MDTA. As courses were established, information about them was disseminated among the former Armour employees, giving a description of courses offered throughout Iowa and Nebraska for which the unemployed workers might be eligible, and explaining application procedures. On a less formal basis, many individuals came directly to the committee office for information and counseling. Eventually, the office became a focal point for aid in dealing with the problems of adjustment in the labor market.

Second, the committee often represented displaced employees seeking acceptance in a particular MDTA course. In view of the committee's experience in Fort Worth there was some concern that the imposition of rigid standards, such as test scores, would exclude many former Armour employees from the benefits of the government program. In extended discussions with state and local employment service officials, it was agreed that there should be a flexible approach to the criteria for accepting trainees in the various MDTA courses. As had occurred elsewhere, with further experience in the administration of MDTA programs, the importance of reaching the "difficult" cases became more generally appreciated.

Although few problems arose in relations with the local employment service office, some difficulties were encountered in the enrollment of former Armour employees in retraining programs controlled by other specialized agencies.

In one case, four women had waited for a year to enter a course for licensed practical nurses. When the class finally opened, two of the applicants were rejected by the administrators of this program on unspecified grounds of "unsuitability." The action appeared capricious, and the committee's representatives protested. When no satisfaction was obtained at the local level, appeals were made to the statewide office of vocational education in Des Moines. The state officials, in their turn, were unable to reverse the decision and tacitly acknowledged that even where the MDTA program was involved, the administration of the nursing course was subject to the autonomous control of the State Nurses' Board, the official agency that regulated the profession in Iowa. Consequently, the Armour employees in question were deprived of this opportunity for training.

Third, the committee developed several programs on its own initiative, supplementing those offered under government auspicies. These programs covered two kinds of situations. On the one hand, efforts were made to help those individuals who clearly did not qualify for MDTA courses; on the other, the committee financed courses in special occupational areas for which government support could not reasonably be expected. Thus the committee's retraining activities were largely residual, filling in gaps left by the government-sponsored programs. For example, the Automation Fund Committee developed a nurses' aide program for poorly educated older women. In addition, one displaced worker with considerable artistic ability was approved for a course in commercial art, and three others were enrolled in college with the ultimate object of obtaining degrees in education and law.

Fourth, the committee's representatives often worked closely with the local officials in the planning and implementation of particular programs. This collaboration took various forms. On a few occasions there was joint planning of a particular course. The committee also helped to find facilities that were not readily available, such as those necessary for a course in retail meatcutting. In another instance, the committee paid for a newspaper advertisement to recruit an instructor for the machinist training course, an expense for which there was no budgetary provision in the federal program. In various ways, the committee sought to support and expedite the government retraining effort.

Finally, the Automation Fund Committee helped to canvass local employers concerning on-the-job training programs, provisions for which are made under the terms of the Manpower Act. This option appeared especially attractive in Sioux City because of the limited vocational education facilities available there. Formal responsibility for developing such programs is lodged with the Bureau of Apprenticeship Training (BAT). However, because one BAT representative, with headquarters in Des Moines, serviced the entire state, little initiative was forthcoming in that quarter. In addition, the paper work involved in establishing on-the-job training under MDTA was formidable enough to discourage most employers, especially if only a handful of trainees were involved. An additional burden was imposed by what appeared to be the excessive time requirements specified by the BAT representative. For example, a mattress manufacturer's enthusiasm for an on-the-job training program quickly dimmed when he was informed that the formal training period should be about two years. He maintained that a competent mattress builder could be trained in the use of modern materials, such as polyfoam, in six months. In any event, no on-the-job programs were instituted under MDTA, and only one program, for a single individual, was started through the unaided efforts of the committee.

Two years after the plant shutdown, 156 persons had entered training in Sioux City. Of this total, 119 were enrolled in MDTA programs and 37 were supported directly by the Armour Automation Fund Committee. In addition, 29 persons had participated in a special literacy class, sponsored and financed by the committee, with the aim of correcting basic educational deficiencies among those enrolled in or contemplating enrollment in a training course. The characteristics of the Sioux City trainees were similar to those of trainees in the earlier projects—that is, about 65 per cent were men and 35 per cent women, the median age of the trainees was approximately 42, and average seniority was fifteen years.

The range of courses encompassed by the Sioux City program was as broad as in Fort Worth. Under MDTA and through the private efforts of the Automation Fund Committee, former Armour workers were enrolled in classes covering welding, machine operation, electronics, radio and TV repair, cosmetology, typing and other office skills, retail meatcutting, automobile repair, commercial art, photography, cooking and baking, mechanical drafting, air conditioning and refrigeration, licensed practical nurse, nurse's aide, and teacher training. A special course was also set up under MDTA for tractor repair and maintenance, reflecting the importance of agriculture in the Sioux City area.

## Facilities and Finances

The establishment of objectives and selection procedures is the necessary first step in beginning a retraining program. These goals and procedures become practical, however, only when adequate training facilities are available, and when financial support for the retrainees is forthcoming. The more ambitious programs impose heavier burdens in terms of both facilities and finances; and, the way in which these burdens are met brings into sharp focus the capacity of the community at large to deal with the problems of major labor displacement.

### Facilities: Breadboards and Bottlenecks

Finding adequate training facilities posed few problems in Oklahoma City. Because the objectives of the program were limited and the courses required generally fell into standard occupational categories, the training needed could usually be satisfied by existing public and private resources. Most of the trainees enrolled in the Adult Institute, a division of the Oklahoma City public school system. The capacity of the Institute was such that no special measures were necessary to accommodate the former Armour workers. The courses that were not available in the public school system were offered by private institutions devoted to more specialized occupations such as cosmetology, air conditioning, and real estate sales and management.

Some initiative was necessary by the committee in the cases of two applicants, an assessment of whose aptitudes and of labor market conditions indicated that they might have prospects in furniture upholstery and in retail meatcutting, respectively. However, there were no courses available in Oklahoma City in either of these subjects. At the request of the committee, the Adult Institute organized a special course in upholstery which was subsequently attended by fifteen retrainees. The retail meatcutting course required greater ingenuity. Special facilities had to be found, meat had to be purchased as "training supplies," and arrangements had to be made for the subsequent sale of the cut meat, if the cost were not to be prohibitive. After considerable search and negotiation the necessary facilities were found and the course was undertaken. It is unlikely that this project would have materialized without the active aid of the Amalgamated Meat Cutters Union's representatives in Oklahoma City.

In Fort Worth, the major difficulty was not one of adequate vocational educational facilities, but rather of making these facilties available to all former Armour workers who sought to enter retraining. As the former site of the Consolidated Aircraft Company, currently a major installation of General Dynamics, Fort Worth had developed a comprehensive and progressive vocational training system to service the needs of local industry. A large, well-equipped public school offered adult training eighteen hours a day in occupations ranging from Diesel mechanic to machinist and electronic technician. As evidence of the excellence of the facilities and staff, the Bureau of Indian Affairs used the Fort Worth school system as a major base for the training of Indians sent to that city from all over the country. In addition to the public facilities, there were several private schools where office occupations, data processing, and some industrial occupations were taught.

This auspicious situation was marred by one overwhelming flaw: almost all public and private facilities were segregated along racial lines, and could not be used by Negroes. Since a substantial proportion of the prospective Armour retrainees were Negroes, this discriminatory policy imposed drastic limitations upon the committee's program. A separate vocational school for Negroes did exist in Fort Worth, but it did not offer the same courses as the school reserved for whites, and gave greater emphasis to such traditional "Negro trades" as shoe repair and woodworking. Moreover, the adult program at the Negro school had been discontinued some time before, and the school authorities were unwilling to reinstitute it on a temporary basis.

Extensive discussions were held with local officials in an effort to find some way to make the public vocational educational facilities available to Negro retrainees. Although these officials expressed general sympathy with the committee's objectives, they stated that they had little discretion in the matter because racial segregation was required by law. A desegregation suit was pending in the federal courts, but this did not provide an immediate solution to the problem. In time, the public vocational educational facilities were desegregated; but the development came too late to be of much help to the committee's program.

As a short-term tactic, the school officials were willing to set up and administer integrated classes away from the public facilities, and for one course, in warehouse management and inventory control, they actually did so. But the more technical courses—which held the promise of greater rewards in the labor market—could not be established on this basis because of the equipment needed. One additional concession made by the school authorities enabled Negro women to enroll in a cosmetology course at the Negro vocational school during the day. At the same time, many of the white trainees did enter evening courses at the then-segregated Institute.

Private institutions also generally adhered to local patterns of discrimination. Some indication of the magnitude of the problem is afforded by the fact that in a city of 400,000 people it was not possible for a Negro woman to receive formal training in office and secretarial skills! One private school for cashiers, checkout clerks, and other occupations related to supermarkets did hold separate classes for Negroes. And, after negotiation with a previously all-white trade school, the committee persuaded the owners to establish an integrated class in air conditioning installation and repair, when it stipulated that a group of fifteen former Armour workers had to be accepted on a nondiscriminatory basis or none would be enrolled at all. Unfortunately, this victory proved a costly one to the committee and the individual trainees, since the quality of instruction provided by the school proved to be substandard.

The limitations of the traditional vocational facilities, both in scope and in freedom of access, prompted the Automation Fund Committee to use or develop facilities that normally were not used for such purposes. A special (integrated) course in food service was established in cooperation with a local church. Instruction in clothes pressing was offered on the premises of a large tailor shop. Goodwill Industries, which usually limits its training activities to handicapped workers, agreed to accept a few Armour employees for particular training courses. And, with the cooperation of a local meat wholesaler and the Amalgamated Meat Cutters Union, another course was instituted in retail meatcutting. These special arrangements helped to fill the gaps in the conventional training facilities, but it should be noted that substantial administrative effort by the committee was needed to organize and supervise such special courses.

The search for adequate facilities also was extended beyond Fort Worth. The school situation in Dallas was more favorable to Negroes than in Fort Worth. A few integrated schools were available in industrial vocational areas, and there was a commercial college for Negro women. Because of distance, however, the Dallas facilities were used only sparingly. Ultimately, four Negroes took training in Dallas—one in electronics, two in welding, and one in secretarial skills.

Resort was also made to out-of-town facilities when highly specialized skills were involved. One man with prior training in general air conditioning wanted additional instruction in truck refrigeration. Through Armour and Company, arrangements were made to send him to a school conducted by a truck refrigeration firm in Minneapolis. While in training, he received $50 a week from the refrigeration firm; the committee's support was limited to transportation costs.

The problems encountered in Sioux City were sharply different from those in Fort Worth. Vocational education facilities in the community were meager and frequently obsolete. Courses available in the local public school system were more or less limited to machine shop techniques, automobile mechanics, and welding. A new area technical school, financed under the provisions of the National Defense Education Act, also offered courses in mechanical drafting and electronics. Besides the narrow range of subjects for which facilities were currently available, there were other deficiencies from the committee's—and the government's—point of view. The public school's equipment generally was out of date, and the faculty had little experience with the kind of program contemplated by the committee. The area technical school, on the other hand, was well equipped and well staffed, but it gave only two-year courses—an excessive period for adult trainees with family obligations. Ultimately, the public school facilities were used for MDTA courses for machinists, welders, and automobile mechanics, but only after new equipment had been provided by the government. Two former Armour workers did enroll in the drafting classes at the area technical school; however, because both had large families, the financial strain was acute.

Private training facilities in Sioux City were equally sparse. They were limited to one barber school, two schools of cosmetology and two "business colleges." MDTA programs for clerk-typists and beauticians were set up in these private institutions. In both, the MDTA trainees merely enrolled in the regular classes.

In order to develop a comprehensive retraining program it was apparent that additional resources were necessary. That financial support was available under MDTA led to some optimism on this count. Prolonged negotiations between government officials and the local school board in the hope of expanding the public school vocational education facilities were fruitless; the board refused to take any additional steps to accommodate the needs of the displaced Armour workers, even though virtually all expenses were to be assumed by the federal government. The main object of contention was a proposed MDTA course in automobile body and fender repair which required a new set of facilities. This episode will be described more fully in Chapter 7.

Blocked by the school board's decision, the MDTA administrators and the Automation Fund Committee's representatives made efforts to establish a regional MDTA training center in an unused building at an Air Force base in the area. Ultimately, this center was intended to serve not only Sioux City but a wide area in Iowa, South Dakota, and Nebraska as well. This plan quickly aborted when the Air Force refused to release the building.

There was now no choice left but to expand training facilities on a piecemeal basis. An MDTA course in retail meatcutting was set up in the cutting room of a large butcher store. The auto body and fender program was finally initiated when the government administrators leased and equipped a suitable building. Similar steps were taken to institute approved courses. Although the committee and government representatives might congratulate themselves on their diligence and ingenuity, all this improvisation was hardly satisfactory. First of all, there is little doubt that the cost of the various programs was significantly higher than if they had been held in an ongoing educational institution, such as the public schools. Second, the establishment of training facilities *de novo* took so long that when a particular course finally was ready to get under way, many of the prospective trainees had lost interest and drifted away to various unskilled jobs.

The committee improvised one course on its own initiative, outside the framework of MDTA. Because of a relatively heavy concentration of hospitals and nursing homes in Sioux City, the local employment service proposed a nurse's aide course, intended particularly for older women or those with major educational deficiencies. When it became apparent that long delays could be expected in moving the proposal through the appropriate government agencies, the committee acted independently, with the cooperation of a large hospital and Goodwill Industries. The curriculum and most of the administrative work associated with the course were handled by a registered nurse employed by Goodwill Industries.

Besides this arduous improvisation, some reliance had to be put on facilities in communities outside Sioux City. Eleven persons were sent to Omaha, about 100 miles away, under the auspices of the Automation Fund Committee. Two other retrainees enrolled in colleges away from home, and six men attended MDTA courses in cities as distant as Topeka, Kansas. The use of out-of-town facilities gave opportunities that would not otherwise have been possible to persons with an intense desire to enter a retraining program. But for most of the displaced workers, the prospect of being away from home and their families for a prolonged period of time sharply reduced the attractiveness of this option.

The Sioux City experience particularly demonstrates the fundamental effect that the amount and quality of vocational education available can have on the ability of a community to adjust to the changing situations of the modern American labor market. Communities content to equate vocational education with making breadboards in shop classes are bound to suffer. Every community might well examine its educational system in the light of probable occupational requirements over the years—including the prospect of an occasional "crash" retraining program.

## Finances and Frugality

The adequacy of the facilities will determine the effective scope of any retraining program; the financial support provided the retrainees will determine, in a large measure, the extent to which the opportunity for training is exploited by those whom the program hopes to reach. The question of finances is obviously important to a group that has been subjected to a drastic reduction of income and whose future prospects are uncertain. The possible financial burdens for a retrainee are twofold. First, there is the cost of the retraining itself. Second, there is the problem of meeting current personal and family expenses during the period of instruction. A further and more subtle consideration is the "opportunity cost" of foregone income from possible employment in lieu of retraining; for although many retrainees would be unemployed in any event, others would undoubtedly find jobs whose potential in the long run might be limited but which would nonetheless provide some current income.

Financial support for the retrainees may take various forms and may be combined in ways varying with the circumstances. Public or private outlays can be made for the cost of the training and other related expenses. Income during the period of training may be obtained through part-time or full-time work on temporary jobs. Unemployment compensation may be available to those who have the necessary record of prior employment. Those who have exhausted their unemployment benefits may be given direct grants in the form of living allowances from public or private sources. Finally, loans can be made available in cases of acute financial need. In the committee's programs, in fact, all of these methods were used to some extent. The emphasis changed, however, as new resources became available and as the philosophy underlying the committee's activities was modified.

At first the committee's response to the question of financial support for the retrainees was cautious and limited. Direct aid to the trainees was restricted to payments for tuition in accordance with a predetermined formula. The Automation Fund Committee paid the first $60 of the cost of a course, plus one-half the balance up to a maximum of $150. In most cases, the application of this formula meant that the committee paid the entire cost, since most students were enrolled in public schools where tuition charges were minimal. In special cases, such as the retail meatcutting class, all expenses were defrayed by the Automation Fund Committee. Nonetheless, because there was a fixed limit on the extent of the committee's contributions in any individual case, the formula established implicit limitations on the scope of the courses selected.

No provision was made for the payment of subsistence allowances to the retrainees from committee funds. Instead, exclusive reliance was placed on public and individual resources. It was anticipated that most of the retrainees could draw unemployment compensation benefits while they were in school. This assumption proved difficult to implement, however. In Oklahoma, as in Texas and Iowa (and over twenty other states), a person enrolled in a daytime training course is not considered "available for work," and is therefore disqualified from receiving unemployment benefits. As a practical expedient, the committee avoided this punitive regulation by scheduling night courses. The night classes also made it somewhat easier for those who had exhausted their benefits to find temporary or part-time employment during the day to provide at least some income while they were in training. On the other hand, evening classes reduced the daily training time and therefore extended the calendar time necessary to complete the course. In addition, several persons undoubtedly violated the letter of the law by filing for unemployment benefits while attending school on a full-time basis. This practice would not be discovered as long as the trainee was not offered a job by the employment service—an unlikely occurrence in view of the state of the local labor market. Thus, the policy governing the payment of benefits to retrainees not only penalized those persons willing to invest their effort in self-improvement, but also encouraged an undesirable attitude toward the law.

The restraint in giving financial aid that prevailed in Oklahoma City was modified in connection with the Fort Worth project, although many of the same problems and restrictions were present. The principal change was in the committee's policy on the payment of tuition. In Fort Worth no formal ceiling was placed on the amount of tuition that could be paid to an individual. The committee approved an initial allotment of $25,000 to finance the over-all retraining project. A canvass was then made to learn something of the demand for training and the distribution of courses before setting any limit on the amount of individual aid. Ultimately, the committee decided to pay full tuition costs in almost every case. These costs averaged $270 per course, and ranged from $50 to $800. Frequently the tuition included sizable payments for tools, books, or other necessary equipment. Travel allowances were given to persons who had to commute to Dallas for a course. The total cost of the program was $45,000; supplementary appropriations were provided by the committee to cover the expenses in excess of the original allotment.

As in Oklahoma City, no subsistence payments were made to the Fort Worth retrainees from committee funds. Again, the greatest reliance was placed upon unemployment compensation and temporary, part-time employment as sources of income to persons in training. Following the Oklahoma City pattern, the receipt of unemployment compensation was complicated by a state administrative ruling that persons engaged in full-time schooling were not "available for employment" and therefore were ineligible for benefits. Consequently, most of the trainees attended evening courses. Also, the duration of many of the courses meant that a substantial proportion of the trainees had exhausted their benefit claims before the completion of the course. To provide some income during this period, an estimated 50 per cent of the male trainees held some part-time or full-time jobs, largely menial and poorly paid.

The problem of obtaining subsistence income while in training caused severe hardship in several cases, and in some instances led to a dropout from the program. One striking example of the hardships undergone by trainees involved a man with a family of nine children. In addition to three hours of training every weekday night, he spent long daytime hours working as a laborer. When his income from this proved inadequate, he sold a number of household effects in an effort to keep going; even so, he was ultimately forced to drop out of the program. In other cases, individual retrainees managed to complete their courses only after dropping out for some period of time to replenish their resources by full-time work.

Financial aid marshaled for the retrainees was most varied and substantial in the Sioux City program, and reflected the direct involvement of the federal government and the continued elaboration of the committee's policies. Under both MDTA and committee-sponsored programs, full tuition costs were paid for all courses. On the average, the committee's expenses were higher in Sioux City than Fort Worth because of the more extensive use of private schools. However, the committee was in a better position to assume these costs since a majority of the Armour trainees entered government programs.

The most significant addition to the financial resources available to retrainees consisted of subsistence allowances. Under the provisions of MDTA, workers enrolled in an approved government course who were also heads of households drew a "training allowance" equal to the average unemployment benefit amount paid in the state in the quarter preceding payment of the allowance. This allowance was payable for a maximum of fifty-two weeks and averaged approximately $32 per week for trainees in Iowa. These allowances had an extremely salutary effect; among other things, they made it possible for trainees to pursue a full-time program without jeopardizing an important source of income. Nonetheless, as originally constituted, the subsistence allowance was not an unmixed blessing. First, allowances were the same for each trainee regardless of the number of dependents. For persons with large families, $32 was generally insufficient support over the long period required to complete many of the courses. Second, if a retrainee sought to augment his income by part-time employment, deductions were made from his allowance on the basis of the number of hours worked.

These deficiencies in the arrangements for the financial support of federal retrainees were partially remedied by two legislative changes which came into effect after the Sioux City program had started. Under these amendments, trainees could work up to twenty hours per week without deductions from the training allowance. In addition, supplementary allowances of $10 per week could be made, based on need and the duration of training. Although more than three months passed before the necessary administrative regulations were drawn up by the Department of Labor, many of the trainees were able to benefit from these permissive amendments.

Two additional financial supplements were provided from the committee's resources. As noted earlier, the inadequacies of training facilities in Sioux City made it necessary for the committee to arrange programs for several retrainees in other cities. In the few cases involved, a travel and living allowance of $35 a week was given to each trainee. This amount was equal to an allotment provided under MDTA for out-of-town courses.

In addition to direct grants for subsistence, the committee also experimented with a loan program analogous to student loan programs used in many universities. Under this program, a local bank agreed to loan up to $1,000 per individual to persons in training who were approved by the Committee, up to a total of $20,000. In return, the committee deposited a $5,000 guarantee fund with the bank. Repayment of the loans did not begin until three months after the borrower had completed his training course. Interest incurred while the borrower was in training was paid from the guarantee fund. Subsequent interest on repayment is at the rate of 5 per cent on the unpaid balance, a rate substantially below the market rate on personal loans.

Participants in the loan program fell into two categories. First were people confronted with some immediate financial crisis, who required aid to continue their training. Second were those who wished to arrange their affairs in order to complete a training program without undue financial pressures, even though their current resources were apparently adequate. To the latter, modest loans were made to prepay utility bills or monthly mortgage installments.

At first the program was administered with extreme prudence. A credit investigation was conducted in each case, and the borrower had to pledge some collateral, even though it might be nominal, with little market value. Applications were rejected in only a few instances, and there was no indication that the retrainees viewed the program as an opportunity to exploit a low-cost source of funds without reference to real needs. Over the course of the Sioux City project fourteen loans were made totaling $6,500. To date, there have been no defaults in repayment and all but two of the loans have been completely repaid.

Public attitudes toward financial aid to unemployed people who are taking training have a puritanical tinge. It is frequently assumed that such aid will promote malingering and subsidize the idle. This judgment appears to be just as erroneous when applied to retraining programs as it has been elsewhere. Training is generally an arduous experience for the unemployed worker, and can scarcely be considered institutionalized malingering. Even with the financial support available to trainees in Sioux City, many men and their families were forced to make genuine sacrifices in order to capitalize on this opportunity for self-improvement. Moreover, the hard economic facts indicate that the price of low support in a lengthy program is a high dropout rate, which wastes the resources already invested from public or private funds and by the trainee himself.

### Administrative Support

Retraining programs are not self-administering. The problems of operating a successful program do not end at the entrance to vocational school, but persist all through the training; and some follow-up is imperative to carry the program to fruition. Continued administrative effort is especially important in dealing with people who had not been in a formal educational situation for many years. In this respect, the women who served as full-time employees of the committee at the site of the project were extremely important in handling day-to-day problems. Offices were invariably maintained on a full-time basis until the training program was well under way, and on a part-time basis for as long as two years after the placement and training program had commenced.

As the programs progressed, problems of morale inevitably arose among trainees who questioned their own ability or will to pursue a particular course to its conclusion. In such cases, the committee's representatives have often engaged in intensive counseling without attempting to subject the individual to a "pep talk." Moral support must often be supplemented by concrete, special-purpose aid in order to be effective. For example, two trainees in a mechanical drafting program were having great difficulty because of their lack of basic physics and mathematics. A tutor was hired at a local college to give them the supplementary instruction they needed. At a more basic level, some retrainees were referred to literacy courses in an effort to improve their performance; and where financial problems were paramount, help was provided to obtain part-time employment.

These supportive measures need to be accompanied by other steps to police the operation of the program. The process of scrutiny applies to both the trainees and the trainers. Inevitably complaints arise concerning the quality of instruction, alleged favoritism, the adequacy of equipment, and so on. They must be investigated; if justified, steps may be taken to rectify the situation. Such problems are most likely to occur when marginal or untried schools are involved; however, difficulties can develop in institutions of demonstrated competence when heavy burdens are placed on existing capacities.

On the other side of the ledger, problems may arise concerning the performance of the trainees. Many were "slow starters," whose initial performance often prompted instructors to recommend dismissal from the program. However, in several cases the committee arranged extended trial periods which gave the trainee an opportunity to adjust more fully to a formal learning situation and to demonstrate his ability to complete the course satisfactorily. Such cases arose most frequently in MDTA courses in Sioux City, where there was limited experience in adult education of this kind. On the other hand, there were a few instances in which a trainee had to be dropped because of unsuitability or excessive absenteeism. In one case, a man who had enrolled in a data-processing course had to withdraw after six weeks when it became clear that he couldn't master the necessary material. In another, more unusual case, a Latin American entered an air conditioning course in Fort Worth with the understanding that he was also to participate in a special class in reading and writing. When he repeatedly refused to attend the literacy course, and his performance in the technical program suffered accordingly, he was dropped from the program. In general, the committee attempted to maintain a permissive attitude toward the retrainees as long as they showed evidence of continued effort at self-improvement.

Aside from individual motivation, two considerations relating to the organization and duration of the training course itself, appeared to influence the trainees' performance. In Fort Worth it was possible to set up many of the courses on a "continuous cycle" basis. As a result, a particular course might not have a fixed calendar schedule, but consisted of a specified number of units of study or practice, each with a range of hours allowed for completion. At any given time, different trainees might be engaged in mastering different units. The "continuous cycle" approach affords considerable flexibility to both administrators and trainees. Some allowance can be made for the differential progress of the trainees; and if an individual must withdraw from the program for a short period because of some personal requirement, he need not abandon it altogether. Moreover, it also becomes possible for trainees to commence at different times rather than as a "cohort class." In Sioux City it was not possible to use this more sophisticated approach, a factor which helps to explain the higher dropout rate in that city than in Fort Worth.

A second consideration was the length of the courses, which was clearly excessive in some cases. In general, this problem was most acute in the licensed trades such as those of barber and beautician. In both Texas and Iowa it takes longer to train a barber than it does a reasonably skilled machine tool operator or secretary. Several of the other, traditional courses have a more leisurely pace, and with some effort could often be shortened without any apparent loss of effectiveness. In Fort Worth, the length of the machinist course was reduced by about one-third, after the vocational teaching staff had been encouraged to accelerate the training program for Armour workers—and for subsequent MDTA retrainees. The machinist course in Sioux City was twice as long as that in Fort Worth. Although there were qualitative differences in the two courses, these differences did not appear to justify the wide time spread. It is obvious that the longer the course, the more likely that a larger proportion of adult retrainees will fall by the wayside.

## The Results of Retraining

The problems of administering a retraining program are significant only in relation to the results. Several standards may be used to evaluate the extent to which a program has achieved the objective of preparing displaced workers for new jobs. The rate of completion is an initial measure of effectiveness. Once the trainee has completed his course, his experience in finding a job is clearly a crucial index of success or failure. Beyond a gross assessment of employment status, more refined judgments may be made concerning the relationship of the jobs held to the content of the training courses and the wages received on these jobs. Finally, qualitative insights can contribute to an over-all assessment of the impact of retraining on the labor market adjustment of the displaced worker.

The process of evaluation is subject to the usual problems of data collection and classification. In addition, differences in circumstances and economic environment often make comparisons difficult. Important questions are also raised concerning the time period most appropriate for analysis. It may be asserted that the value of retraining, as a form of "investment in human resources," is revealed only over a long period of time, and not in the first year or two following the completion of the program. Within these acknowledged limitations, nonetheless, administrative requirements posed by the immediate problems of large-scale displacement require some short-term assessment.

## Completions and Dropouts

As Table 8 indicates, a substantial majority of those who entered retraining in all three of the programs conducted by the Automation Fund Committee successfully completed their courses of study. However, there was a significant difference in

TABLE 8. EXPERIENCE IN TRAINING

|  | Started Training | Completed Training | Dropouts | Dropouts: Per cent of Total |
|---|---|---|---|---|
| Oklahoma City | 58 | 52 | 6 | 10.3 |
| Fort Worth | 168[a] | 150 | 18 | 10.7 |
| Sioux City | 156 | 126[b] | 30 | 19.2 |

[a] Does not include two persons who started training but who died shortly after the completion of their courses.

[b] Nineteen persons were still in training in Sioux City as of July, 1965. It was expected that all of these trainees would complete their courses.

the dropout rates in Oklahoma City and Fort Worth on the one hand, and in Sioux City on the other. In the first two cities the proportion of dropouts was approximately 10 per cent; in the latter, it was nearly twice as high.

This difference probably can be explained by variations in the organization and administration of the three programs. In Oklahoma City the criteria for acceptance into the program were stringent and the courses were generally of short duration, so that few trainees would fall by the wayside because of extreme financial difficulties or inability to master the required material. In fact, most of the dropouts were women who appeared to lose interest shortly after they entered retraining.

But the same factors cannot explain the wide spread between the dropout rates observed in Fort Worth and Sioux City. In both cities the admission standards were highly flexible and many of the courses were of long duration. In Sioux City, most of the retrainees received MDTA training allowances, whereas in Fort Worth, the retrainees received no special financial aid from either the government or the Automation Fund Committee. Theoretically, this difference should have enhanced the comparative performance of the Sioux City program. Obviously, other factors were at work.

First, the use of the "continuous cycle" approach in Fort Worth made it possible for trainees to withdraw temporarily from the program for personal reasons without making withdrawal irrevocable. Conversely, the MDTA courses in Sioux City generally operated on a fixed schedule, so that any short-term problem was likely to result in a dropout or disqualification. At the same time, the "continuous cycle" made it possible for highly motivated individuals to accelerate the pace of their efforts and thus shorten the training period. In Fort Worth, about 10 per cent of the trainees finished their courses in less than the designated number of hours. Again, the more formal arrangements in Sioux City generally did not permit this option.

Second, the differential dropout rates between Sioux City and Fort Worth reflect different arrangements for the financial support of the trainees in the two projects. Paradoxically, the direct training allowance provided under MDTA probably served to increase the number of people who withdrew from the programs in Sioux City. Under the formula used, all trainees who were heads of households received a flat sum of from $30 to $32 regardless of the number of dependents. This amount frequently was inadequate for persons with heavy family responsibilities. Moreover, efforts to increase current income through part-time employment would be penalized by deductions from the government allowance. Even when this limitation was relaxed in March, 1963, part-time employment was not feasible for many trainees because of the scheduling of the courses.

In Fort Worth, by contrast, many trainees were eligible for unemployment compensation benefits because the courses were mostly held in the evening, so that they could still be considered "available for work." The amount of the benefits received varied with the number of dependents, up to a specified maximum. Also, were a retrainee to exhaust his claims, the same scheduling arrangements made it easier for him to find and accept temporary employment. As indicated earlier, a substantial proportion of the male trainees in Fort Worth held some kind of job while enrolled in the program.

This analysis does not support the inference that government subsistence allowances *per se* will increase the dropout rate in a training program. Instead, it focuses attention on the importance of ensuring that such support, when it is given, is adequate to the needs of the retrainees and does not carry conditions which penalize supplementary efforts at self-help. At the same time, these efforts at self-help can, and probably should, be facilitated by taking into account such elementary considerations as the daily scheduling of instruction.

Third, the higher dropout rate in Sioux City stemmed in part from a lack of coordination in administering the over-all committee program. That is, the retrainees were persons who had elected not to exercise their rights under the interplant transfer plan. This decision, in turn, had been affected by the nature of the available alternatives. However, as explained in an earlier chapter, after the initial decisions had been made, transfer rights were extended to jobs at a new plant in West Point, Nebraska. When the displaced Sioux City workers were given a second opportunity to transfer, several persons who had already enrolled in a training course elected to drop out and take a job at West Point. The situation was further complicated when some of these transferees reacted negatively to their new jobs and quickly exercised their "flow-back" rights in order to re-enter training! Clearly, a program to handle large-scale displacement will generate its own problems when the options available to those who are displaced are ambiguous or change at different stages of the decision-making process.

The analysis of the experience of the former Armour workers in training casts some light on the subtleties of administering such programs. Retraining is not an automatic process; rather, it requires painstaking attention to the supporting arrangements and the conduct of the courses. Perhaps the most significant observation to be made from this phase of the committee's experience is that so few dropouts occurred while the committee—and the government officials—were feeling their way.

## Experience in the Labor Market

The completion of a retraining program is only a means toward the overriding objective of obtaining new employment in the labor market. An ornate diploma is scant solace to the displaced worker who is still without a job. The employment experience of the retrainees who completed their courses successfully in the three cities is shown in Table 9. Comparisons should be made here with

TABLE 9. EMPLOYMENT EXPERIENCE OF RETRAINEES

|  | Oklahoma City[a] | Fort Worth[b] | Sioux City[c] |
|---|---|---|---|
| Employed | 42 | 135 | 90 |
| Unemployed | 5 | 3 | 17 |
| Actively Seeking Work | } 5 | 1 | 10 |
| Intermittently Seeking Work | | 2 | 2 |
| Out of the Labor Force | 5 | 12 | 5 |

[a] Approximately 18 months after completion of courses.
[b] Approximately 1 year–18 months after completion of courses.
[c] Approximately 3–12 months after training.

caution. Differences in the state of the local labor market, in the characteristics of the retrainees, in the occupational focus of the training, and in the duration of the post-training experience to be measured, all present obstacles to comparability. Nonetheless, the data do provide at least a preliminary basis for evaluating the committee's efforts.

Of the three projects, the best employment record clearly was registered in Fort Worth. There, 97.8 per cent of those who completed training *and who were active in the labor market* were employed within a year to eighteen months following the completion of their courses. In Oklahoma City, 89.4 per cent of the job-seekers were working eighteen months after completing training; and in Sioux City 88.2 per cent were employed within three to twelve months after completion. It is significant that the unemployment rate of the Sioux City retrainees was as high as 36 per cent in the period before the cutoff date used for the data in Table 9.

The relationships among the three cities are altered slightly if employment is calculated in proportion to the total number of persons who completed training, including those who subsequently withdrew from the labor market on a permanent or temporary basis. Calculated thus, the employment rates are 90 per cent for Fort Worth, 84.1 per cent in Sioux City, and 80.8 per cent in Oklahoma City. The significance of these figures lies in the reasons for not seeking work. It is often maintained that job-seekers withdraw from the labor market because they perceive very dim prospects for employment, and that if jobs are available, they will seize the opportunity to work. For the greater part, this generalization does not seem applicable to the Armour retrainees. In Fort Worth, two of the twelve persons who were "out of the labor market" were men who suffered from a temporary physical disability. The other ten were women, most of whom were secondary breadwinners in their families. Obviously, these women had taken retraining from a mixture of motives—partly to avail themselves of a "good thing," partly as insurance upon which they could draw if family finances required. Similarly, all of the trainees who had withdrawn from the labor market in Oklahoma City were women. The Sioux City experience, on the other hand, is somewhat different; four of the five persons not seeking work were men. However, most of these withdrawals were attributed to short-term factors such as illness.

A more rigorous evaluation is to compare the employment experience of the retrainees with that of a group of workers drawn from the same population, who did not undertake any training. Such data are available for Fort Worth and Sioux City, where

TABLE 10. EMPLOYMENT STATUS OF MALE TRAINEES COMPLETED AND MALE NONTRAINEES, FORT WORTH, SUMMER 1963
(In Parentheses: Percentage Unemployed in Each Race-Age Bracket)

R = Trainees who had completed training
NR = Nontrainees

| AGE | WHITE Employed | | Unemployed | | NEGRO Employed | | Unemployed | | LATIN Employed | | Unemployed | |
|---|---|---|---|---|---|---|---|---|---|---|---|---|
| | R | NR | R | NR | R | NR | R | NR | R | NR | R | NR |
| Under 30 | 2 | — | 0 (0) | — | — | — | — | — | — | — | — | — |
| 31–40 | 20 | 14 | 0 (0) | 1 (7) | 7 | 11 | 0 (0) | 4 (27) | 7 | 6 | 0 (0) | 3 (33) |
| 41–50 | 6 | 13 | 2 (25) | 5 (28) | 5 | 13 | 0 (0) | 2 (13) | 6 | 10 | 0 (0) | 2 (17) |
| 51–60 | 6 | 12 | 0 (10) | 12 (50) | 3 | 8 | 0 (0) | 7 (47) | 0 | 1 | 0 (0) | 1 (17) |
| Over 60 | 1 | 3 | 0 (0) | 16 (84) | 0 | 3 | 1 (100) | 8 (73) | 0 | 0 | 0 (0) | 1 (100) |
| TOTAL | 35 | 42 | 2 | 34 | 15 | 35 | 1 | 21 | 13 | 17 | 0 | 7 |

surveys were taken by the committee in the summers of 1963 and 1964 to determine the status of former Armour workers who had not transferred, retired, or entered training. In each of these surveys, a random sampling had been made of workers in these categories. It was a simple matter to compare their employment status with that of those who had completed training and who were in the labor market at approximately the same time.

The results of these comparisons, for Fort Worth and Sioux City, are presented in Tables 10 and 11. In both cities, the com-

TABLE 11. EMPLOYMENT STATUS OF MALE TRAINEES COMPLETED AND
MALE NONTRAINEES; SIOUX CITY, SUMMER 1964
(In Parentheses: Percentage Unemployed in Each Age Bracket)

R = Trainees who had completed training
NR = Nontrainees

| | ALL DISPLACED WORKERS SURVEYED | | | |
| AGE | Employed | | Unemployed | |
| | R | NR | R | NR |
| --- | --- | --- | --- | --- |
| Under 30 | 5 | — | 1 (16) | — |
| 31–40 | 8 | 32 | — (0) | 9 (22) |
| 41–50 | 18 | 40 | 6 (25) | 9 (18) |
| 51–60 | 8 | 27 | 2 (20) | 19 (41) |
| Over 60 | — | — | 1 (100) | — |
| TOTAL | 39 | 99 | 10 | 37 |

parisons are restricted to males because of the great variability of participation by women in the labor market. Separate classifications are used for different age groups so as to control the possible effect of this variable, and also for race and ethnic groups in Fort Worth, where a sizable proportion of both the trainees and nontrainees could expect to meet discriminatory barriers in the labor market.

The Fort Worth comparisons reveal significant differences in the employment status of the nontrainees and those who had completed training by the summer of 1963. In every race-age cell but one, the record was better for those who had participated in the committee's program. The differences were particularly dramatic among the Negro and Latin American workers; virtually all of the retrainees were employed, whereas the incidence of joblessness was pronounced among the nontrainees in these racial and ethnic categories. The over-all unemployment rate at the time was 4.5 per cent for the male trainees and 40 per cent for the nontrainees. If all persons over 60 years of age are excluded from the nontrainee group on the grounds that they introduce an upward bias to the findings, the unemployment rate is 28 per cent, still a high figure and more than five times the jobless rate for the retrainees.

An observation not indicated in Table 10 further dramatizes the difference in the employment status of the trainees and nontrainees in Fort Worth. At the time of the survey, twenty of the nontrainees were self-employed whereas only two of the trainees fell into this category. For most of these persons, self-employment appeared to be a last grasp at making a living rather than a realization of the "American dream"—a marginal occupation involving long hours and low pay, such as leasing a gas station, selling door-to-door, hauling dirt, or buying and selling used furniture.

It may be contended that the difference in the experience of the two groups really reflects factors that can't be controlled by reference to broad demographic considerations such as age and race. Thus, participation in the training program may be subject to a process of self-selection whereby the highly motivated individuals, who are most likely to find employment in any event, seize the opportunity for retraining, whereas the nonretrainees are largely persons who lack initiative and will suffer accordingly in the labor market. Without elaborate psychological testing there is no way to prove or disprove this statement. There are, however, no *prima facie* reasons to expect such gross subjective differences between the members of the two groups. Indeed, the nontrainees contained a larger proportion of former craftsmen in the plant, who might be expected to find a more cordial reception in the labor market at large.

For Sioux City the evidence is less persuasive. Here the aggregate unemployment rate of the sample nonretrainees was 28 per cent, whereas it was 20 per cent for the males who had completed their training. The difference is made less significant, however, by the relatively small number of the retrainees. Also, the nonretrainees enjoyed a more favorable employment experience than the retrainees in the important 41–50 age bracket. On the other hand, the younger retrainees, from 31 to 40 years of age, and those in the 51–60 age group, fared better than those who sought employment without attempting to improve their skill.

The comparative experience in Sioux City doubtless was influenced to a large extent by the timing of the survey. Most of the nontrainees had been active in the labor market for nearly a year, whereas the bulk of the retrainees had completed their courses within the previous three months. In Sioux City, as opposed to Fort Worth, delays in launching the project reduced the span of the labor market experience of the retrainees, even though the surveys in both cities were taken about a year after the major displacement occurred. The significant improvement in the employment experience of the Sioux City retrainees noted in Table 9 gives some credence to the assumption that with the passage of time the differential impact of retraining might be more perceptible.

## Job Content and Retraining

Thus far, the relative effectiveness of retraining has been analyzed in terms of completion rates and the general employment record of the retrainees. An additional basis for evaluation may be provided by comparing the content of the jobs with that of the training course. Such data are available on a systematic basis for Fort Worth and Sioux City, and are presented in Table 12. The categories "directly related" and "unrelated" are

TABLE 12. JOB CONTENT AND RETRAINING

| Relation of Job Content to Training | Fort Worth[a] | | Sioux City[b] | |
|---|---|---|---|---|
| Directly related | 48 | | 50 | |
| (% of total employed) | | (35.5) | | (55.6) |
| Indirectly related | 31 | | 4 | |
| (% of total employed) | | (23.0) | | (4.4) |
| Unrelated | 56 | | 36 | |
| (% of total employed) | | (41.5) | | (40.0) |
| TOTAL | 135 | | 90 | |

[a] As of August, 1964.
[b] As of June, 1965.

self-explanatory. The "indirectly related" classification includes those cases in which the retrainee used his specific skills some of the time on the job, or in which his training gave general support to his employment activities. For example, this category included a person who had taken a combination welding course and who used his new skills frequently, but not exclusively, in his job as a millwright. Similarly, a salesman who used his newly acquired skills in bookkeeping and typing to keep records and thus to improve his efficiency was also classified as "indirectly related." In any event, it should be recognized that many of the judgments were arbitrary, and that of necessity they were based primarily on information provided by the retrainees.

As indicated in Table 12, 58.5 per cent of the employed retrainees in Fort Worth held jobs that were directly or indirectly related to the occupational content of their training courses. If the analysis is limited to those in the "directly related" category, the proportion declines to 35.5 per cent. At the same time, well over one-third of the retrainees had taken jobs with no relation at all to the previous training. These results are cast in sharper relief when it is noted that a survey conducted about one year earlier indicated that 52 per cent of the employed retrainees were in jobs directly related, and 63 per cent in jobs either directly or indirectly related, to the training. An examination of individual cases further supports the inference that as time passed, some people shifted from jobs that were training-related to those that did not utilize their new skills.

Several factors contributed to the failure—or unwillingness—of a substantial proportion of the Fort Worth trainees to use their skills in subsequent employment. One was discrimination in the labor market. Thus, 80 per cent of the employed, white male retrainees had jobs directly or indirectly related to their training, whereas only 60 per cent of the Latin Americans and 40 per cent of the Negroes fell in this category. In addition, the fact that many of the Negroes had to enroll in schools where they received inferior instruction reduced the likelihood that they could build up their skills to the levels required by prospective employers. In any event, it is clear that the Negro retrainees, in particular, suffered from special handicaps in developing and utilizing their full occupational capabilities.

Second, the ambitious upgrading attempted in many cases in Fort Worth probably affected the relation between job content and training. Although this observation runs counter to most commonsense evaluations of current labor demand, it can be explained in terms of market operation and organization—that is, a displaced worker who trained for a skilled occupation such as electronics technician usually acquired only marginal competence in the field, and lacked the on-the-job experience frequently demanded by employers when hiring skilled technicians. That a retrainee was over 40 also did not enhance his prospects. Moreover, moving into the ranks of the skilled workers generally meant that the former Armour employee had to shift to sectors of the labor market about which he had limited information, which in turn inhibited his search for an appropriate job. Consequently, those with training for skilled occupations were less likely to obtain training-related employment than those who had set more modest objectives.

Third, following an initial failure to obtain a training-related job, a worker was reluctant to follow up any subsequent opportunities calling for his newly acquired skills. Several persons who had found unrelated jobs failed to follow up such leads from the committee and other sources, but chose instead to keep the jobs they had. Inertia, uncertainty, and the usual range of factors favoring immobility obviously overbalanced any anticipated gains from a job more closely related to training. Ideally, then, intensive efforts to place the retrainees on appropriate jobs should begin before the worker ventures out into the labor market. Otherwise, a cautious self-interest may cause him to retain any job which affords some income and security.

This line of reasoning does not help to explain those cases in which the Fort Worth retrainees did change employment to take jobs that were *unrelated* to the occupational content of their training. The causal factors here were more direct. Several persons who had obtained jobs utilizing their skills moved to other positions when their former jobs proved either too demanding or unrewarding, or both. Thus several practical nurses, who generally experienced no difficulty in finding employment in that field, left it because of the physical effort and peculiar schedules involved. Similarly, a few people who had been trained and employed as barbers and beauticians moved to other fields when their net incomes declined below tolerable levels. It is clear that the process of labor allocation does not stop with completion of a training program.

The Sioux City data reveal that 56 per cent of those who have completed retraining and who are employed have found jobs that are directly related to the content of the course of instruction. The results to date are more impressive when it is noted that nine of the retrainees who are working in jobs unrelated to training returned to work for Armour and Company when new transfer options opened up in West Point, Nebraska, and Worthington, Minnesota.[2] If these individuals are omitted from the calcula-

---

[2] Eleven retrainees returned to Armour. Two were using their new skills.

tions, the proportion of those with training-related jobs is raised to 62 per cent, or nearly double the rate in Fort Worth.

Whatever significant difference there is in the Fort Worth and Sioux City results is largely due to the role of the public employment service. As noted in an earlier chapter, the local employment service office carried out an intensive placement effort for the displaced Armour workers. The Sioux City retrainees, most of whom were enrolled in MDTA programs, were the focus of special measures that were initiated before they completed their courses; whereas the processing by the local employment service office in Fort Worth had been merely routine.

Although the Sioux City results to date are more promising than those in Fort Worth, there is still considerable latitude for improvement. The fact that 40 per cent of the retrainees were not employing their new skills probably reflects basic limitations in the local labor market. In a labor market the size of Sioux City, the capacity to absorb even a small number of additional workers in relatively narrow occupational categories is soon exhausted. This limitation also helps to explain the small proportion of retrainees falling into the "indirect" classification. Without the varied range of opportunities found in a large, complex market the use of any particular skill is likely to become an all-or-nothing proposition. For this reason, the Automation Fund Committee pressed for the quick implementation of the relocation provisions of the amended Manpower Development and Training Act. Again, this effort floundered in a morass of inactivity on the part of the responsible government officials.

In reviewing the experience of the Armour retrainees there is the danger that excessive emphasis will be placed on the relation of the jobs held to the specific content of the training course. To be sure, these relationships cast some light on the extent to which the program has realized its immediate purpose. However, some "slippage" is inevitable as changes take place in individual preferences and the state of the labor market. The broader objectives of retraining are to stimulate the displaced worker to participate actively in the market, and to provide resources that will help him adjust to new circumstances over a long period of time. Elusive as these considerations may be, they should serve as the backdrop to any short-term evaluation of the relation of job content and training.

### Earnings Experience

Whether or not a job is "training-related," most commentators would agree that what it pays is an important criterion for evaluating the effectiveness of retraining. There are several bases for evaluation. The earnings of the retrainees in their present jobs may be compared to those they received at Armour, or the experiences of the retrainees may be compared with those of employed nontrainees, or an assessment may be made of the wage progression of the retrainees over a period of time.

If the first of these is used, the results are unambiguous: In almost all cases the retrainees earned substantially less in their new jobs than they did while employed by Armour. No systematic data are available for Oklahoma City; however, eighteen months after the retraining project had been concluded, Professor Young reported that "almost without exception these workers [the employed retrainees] had jobs that paid less than the wages they had received in the meatpacking plant."

The same conclusion may be drawn from the earnings data for the Fort Worth and Sioux City retrainees, presented in Table 13. At the time of the shutdowns in these two cities the

TABLE 13. AVERAGE HOURLY EARNINGS OF EMPLOYED RETRAINEES

|  | Men | | Women | |
|---|---|---|---|---|
| *Fort Worth* | (1963) | (1964) | (1963) | (1964) |
| All Retrainees | $1.61 | $1.75 | $1.07 | $1.17 |
| White | 1.76 | 1.91 | 1.12 | 1.34 |
| Negro | 1.32 | 1.46 | 1.02 | 1.02 |
| Latin American | 1.56 | 1.74 | .90 | 1.22 |
| *Sioux City* (1965) | | $1.75 | | $1.20 |

NOTE: The Fort Worth data for 1963 are based on a study of 91 persons; for 1964, 135. The Sioux City figures cover 89 persons.

average hourly wage in the Armour plants was between $2.60 and $2.70, with a minimum of $2.45. Using the $2.45 minimum as the base, the average decline in earnings was 25 to 35 per cent for men and 50 to 60 per cent for women.[3] Even so, they are understated since they do not take fringe benefits into account. In 1964 these benefits amounted to $1.06 per hour under the Armour contract. Although no precise quantitative comparisons can be made, it is clear that few of the retrainees found jobs that had fringe benefits equivalent to those included in the labor agreement between Armour and the meatpacking unions.

There was also considerable variation in the experience of different elements in the retrainee group. As indicated above, women fared considerably worse than men. Moreover, for the members of minority groups at Fort Worth, the decrease in earnings was more precipitous than for retrainees who did not face discriminatory barriers. Thus, the average hourly earnings of Negroes and Latin Americans were consistently below those of the white retrainees. Some of these differences may reflect differences in education and in the nature of the retraining programs selected. It is also clear, however, that the segregation of the Fort Worth labor market limited the range of economic opportunities of members of minority groups.[4] For example, Negroes who completed the air-conditioning and meatcutting courses were unable to find work in these occupations, whereas several white retrainees were hired for just such positions.

The influence of discriminatory barriers in the labor market is further revealed by a comparison of the earnings of the retrainees and a sample of nontrainees who were surveyed in the summer of 1963. As shown in Table 14, the average earnings of male train-

[3] The data for figures for Armour and post-training jobs are not exactly comparable since average wages are used for the former but not for the latter. This discrepancy tends to improve the relative position of the retrainees.
[4] It is significant that Latin Americans generally scored as well as or better than whites on the General Aptitude Test Battery, but earned consistently less than the white retrainees. On the average, Negroes scored below the other groups and had less formal education.

ees were consistently higher than those of the nontrainees for each of the racial or ethnic groups involved. On the other hand, the gap between Negro and Latin American trainees and nontrainees cannot be considered significant, whereas a substantial difference did exist between the earnings of whites on the basis of participation in the committee's retraining program. As shown earlier, Negro and Latin American retrainees had a markedly better employment record than the nontrainees in the same subgroups. But it is axiomatic that without free entry to all sectors of the labor market the full benefits of investment in new skills cannot be realized.

Those participating in the committee's retraining programs in Sioux City also fared better in terms of earnings than nontrainees. The difference for men was not a large one, amounting to about $2 per week on the average. It must be borne in mind, however, that the survey of employment and earnings was made during the summer months when highly paid jobs in construction were held by some of the nontrainees. For women the difference was greater, with the trainees earning about $10 per week, or 25 per cent more than the very low wages of employed nontrainees.

Data on the earnings experience of the trainees over longer periods of time are available only for Fort Worth, and are presented in Table 13. Although the number of persons involved is

TABLE 14. AVERAGE HOURLY EARNINGS OF MALE TRAINEES AND
NONTRAINEES, BY RACE, FORT WORTH

|  | Retrainees | Nontrainees |
|---|---|---|
| White | $1.76 | $1.62 |
| Negro | 1.32 | 1.27 |
| Latin American | 1.56 | 1.53 |

too small to support any broad generalizations, the apparent improvement in the economic status of the retrainees is impressive. In one year the earnings of the entire group rose by about 10 per cent. This gain was shared by all elements except the Negro women. Conversely, the white and Latin American women registered above-average increases in earnings. In the intervening year, labor market conditions had improved considerably in Fort Worth, and apparently the employed retrainees were in a good position to capitalize on the change in economic climate. Consequently, their average earnings increased more rapidly than those of workers in the Fort Worth labor market as a whole.[5]

The concepts of "success" and "failure" are inherently ambiguous and cannot be applied to the results of the Automation Fund Committee's retraining efforts with any precision. It is sufficient to note that to date most displaced workers who have enrolled in such programs have seen them through to completion and found some remunerative employment. Where open access to the different sectors of the labor market is maintained there is a reasonable expectation that in time the retrainees will have an opportunity to utilize their new skills and augment their earnings. In general, the retrainees appear to fare better in the market than their peers who have chosen to forego additional formal training. Whether this evaluation points to "success" is largely a normative question. But it seems safe to assert that retraining for displaced workers is one promising point of departure in what is often a long and arduous process of adjustment.

## Retraining the Unemployed: An Overview

The retraining of unemployed workers is a relatively new development in the United States. Although short-term evaluations are risky and may be misleading, some stock-taking is in order for both policymakers and administrators. The absence of firm guides to action in this area means that, at this point, the lessons of pragmatic experiments may be more valuable than any general theory. A few brief observations may be made, although un-

[5] Between July, 1963 and July, 1964 the average hourly earnings of production workers in manufacturing in Fort Worth rose from $2.44 to $2.56, an increase of 5 per cent. *Employment and Earnings*, U. S. Department of Labor, September, 1964.

doubtedly they will be revised as further experience with retraining the unemployed is accumulated.

First, it does seem feasible to retrain displaced workers who have limited educational and occupational backgrounds. Such training may not result in immediately high earnings, but it does seem to help in finding a new job and in giving a new occupational orientation. Thus a retraining program may be viewed as a "staging area" for the labor market. With basic educational backgrounds and sufficient individual motivation, many displaced workers can successfully complete training programs covering a wide range of occupational skills. However, to realize this potential, expert instruction must be available, along with a willingness to adapt that instruction to the special needs and problems of the retrainees.

Second, the availability of adequate vocational educational facilities is a basic requirement for an effective training program. The Fort Worth project was severely limited by artificial deficiencies in the facilities available to Negroes. As a result, the committee used certain private institutions that proved wholly unsatisfactory. In Sioux City, the effectiveness of the program was impaired by the paucity of educational resources. The necessary improvisation caused long delays, which meant that many displaced workers were foreclosed from retraining opportunities. Not every community can sustain a comprehensive vocational educational facility, but those with a large stake in industrial activity should give it a high priority. Smaller communities of necessity will have to draw on resources mobilized over wider political units.

Third, a training program must proceed by stages. The first step should be an investigation of the local labor market and existing training facilities, followed by careful counseling and supervision of the trainee while he is enrolled in the program. Adequate provision must be made for income while in training—either through direct grants or by organizing the program to permit substantial efforts at self-help through part-time and temporary employment. Placement efforts should be considered an integral part of retraining, and preparations for those efforts should be made while the training is in process. By the same token, systematic placement activities may have to continue well beyond the time when the bulk of the trainees have completed their courses. The probability of success in any program to aid displaced workers is greater if these various phases are identified from the outset and integrated into a general manpower plan for the group involved.

Last, it must be recognized that any retraining program geared to the labor market at large represents a calculated risk to both the sponsoring agency and the retrainees. Neither party has control over the vital conditions of demand—conditions that can crown a slipshod program with success, or turn the best-administered program into an exercise in futility. Nonetheless, the evidence indicates that whatever the state of the labor market, those who broaden their basic skills and maintain a capacity to adjust will improve their chances of finding new and satisfactory employment. In an environment characterized by uncertainty, each individual must exploit his opportunities as they arise. Programs for retraining constitute an additional opportunity open to displaced workers, and as such may promise returns substantially above the private and public costs incurred.

# 7 Private Programs and the Public

Response: Complementary Patterns

of Resources and Responsibilities

MAJOR shifts in the geographical distribution of industrial activity—and in employment opportunities—are a common occurrence in a dynamic economy. Acceptance of the inevitability of change does not mean, however, a passive acceptance of the undesirable consequences of such adjustments. There have been significant developments in the pattern of response to the dislocations arising from change. In the past, the withdrawal of a company from a community was generally carried out with abrupt efficiency. Typically, the outmoded facilities were made available to any enterprise that could be attracted, but the legacy of labor displacement was borne by the community alone, within the framework of "automatic" market forces.

In recent years, companies have responded to pressures of conscience, collective bargaining, and public relations by assuming a more active role in helping the workers and the community to deal with the problems of economic change. Coincidentally, the federal government has made a major commitment to action on a wide front. The Manpower Development and Training Act, the Area Redevelopment Act, the Trade Expansion Act and the Economic Opportunity Act all testify to an intense interest in the plight of the unemployed and the community in which they live. Thus, the community is less likely to be left to its own resources in coping with mass displacement. Instead, it can draw on the financial strength and professional competence of governmental and private groups with whom it has a natural reciprocity of interests.

The effective use of these new resources and institutions is no more automatic than the operation of market forces. The more ambitious programs involve problems of communication and co-ordination, and frequently generate tensions among the interested parties. An effective community program, therefore, must resolve these problems of coordination in a manner that recognizes the comparative advantages of the participating agencies and permits the best utilization of resources for the benefit of the individuals most directly affected, the displaced workers. Such well-coordinated working relations will not emerge from abstract administrative planning. Hard decisions must be made about priorities among both the displaced workers and other groups in the community with competing claims to the control and use of some part of the new resources. The process of resolving these claims will, in turn, touch upon fundamental attitudes and values held in the community, which cannot but affect any program that is undertaken.

## The Evolution of Experience: New Places and New Programs

The four major projects initiated by the Automation Fund Committee took shape in diverse community settings. Moreover, as the scope and emphasis of these programs changed, the relations between the committee, the particular community, and the various governmental agencies were also modified. In some situations, involvement in the community was minimal; in others it was complicated and sometimes delicate. From these experiences the committee derived not a set of "principles," but an awareness of the need for a conscious strategy in integrating its limited programs with the resources of the community as a whole.

Although the Oklahoma City project was a modest one and the committee's involvement with the community was minimal, this experience hinted at the difficulties of coordination and priority that were likely to develop in more ambitious programs. A broader arena for the identification and resolution of these problems was provided by the succeeding cases.

*Fort Worth*

The Fort Worth project brought the Automation Fund Committee into close contact with a variety of community agencies. First of all, the plant shutdown involved twice as many workers as in Oklahoma City, necessitating more extensive activities by the committee. Second, a firm commitment had been made to placement and occupational retraining. Third, the Manpower Development and Training Act had been passed, and questions arose concerning possible benefits under this law. Inevitably, then, contacts between the committee and community groups and governmental agencies were more frequent and more crucial to the administration of the project.

From the outset of the program, systematic contacts were made with agencies in Fort Worth that might help achieve the committee's objectives. In order to give a "hometown" flavor to the project and to establish a tripartite basis for administration, the initial contacts were made by a team composed of union and management representatives and the "public" project director.

The team's general approach was to state the goals of the committee, indicate the framework of the program, and solicit suggestions and cooperation. The Chamber of Commerce pledged aid in gaining entry to the Fort Worth business community and in receiving general encouragement, if not support, for the efforts that were under way. The officials of the local school system acted with dispatch in opening their courses to Armour retrainees. Some courses were redesigned to meet the special requirements of this group. The employment service offered a full range of normal counseling and testing services. Arrangements were made with the Dallas office of the Texas Employment Commission, so that a coordinated placement effort could be undertaken in that city as well. Contacts were also made with charitable agencies such as Goodwill Industries and local church groups, whose resources could be used in particular cases.

On the whole, the cooperation of local community and government groups extended to the committee was excellent, especially on those measures that fell within their normal discretion and routines of operation. There were some disappointments, however, where special actions on the part of some community and governmental groups were called for. The principal problems arose from a clash between the dominant values and legal arrangements in the community and the objectives of the committee.

The most sensitive issue involved training opportunities for Negroes. At the time, the school system in Fort Worth was segregated by law. School officials did take steps to set up two integrated classes where small numbers were involved and the capital requirements were small. However, when action was called for on major vocational courses such as those for training machinists, welders, and automobile mechanics, and in air conditioning, the local school administrators were unable or unwilling to provide integrated facilities or set up special classes for Negroes. This outcome was all the more acutely disappointing since at one stage of the discussions with the committee's representatives it was suggested that an integrated class convened on private property but operated by the public school system might be a method of overcoming the legal barriers.

At one point during the prolonged deliberations on this issue, the committee considered legal action against the Forth Worth school system to force equal access to public training facilities. However, when it learned that a suit already had been litigated and that the school board was under a court order to develop a plan for integration, the committee shifted its interest to the details of the plan. There was some cause for satisfaction in that the plan as approved called for an unusual pattern of desegregation, starting at one end with the first grade and at the other with evening vocational education for adults. Ultimately, a few displaced Negroes were able to take advantage of the newly opened facilities, but for many others the change came too late in the readjustment process to be useful.

The difficulty of finding training opportunities for Negroes led the committee to use a private vocational school, which proved wholly unsatisfactory. Since the reputation of the school cast some doubt on the quality of its offerings, special steps were taken to draw up a contract with performance clauses and to provide for close supervision of the trainee's progress. These safeguards were ineffective, however, and the class was canceled several months before the scheduled termination date. Complaints were registered with the Better Business Bureau and the Texas Education Agency, both of which indicated that under existing legal arrangements nothing could be done to rectify the situation or give satisfaction to the trainees.

In general, the problem of controlling the quality of private vocational training is one of importance to displaced workers who are exploring new vocational possibilities. Workers who are unemployed as the result of a conspicuous event such as a plant shutdown are frequently solicited by training schools of dubious quality, which may lead in the end to little more than disappointment and the dissipation of personal resources. The committee's representatives expended considerable energy in persuading workers that courses in motel management or airlines dispatching were inappropriate to their situation.

The committee's efforts to induce unemployed workers in Fort Worth to explore job openings in nearby Dallas also touched a sensitive nerve, when a letter on the subject sent by the committee to former Armour workers was seized upon by the press as a depreciation of Fort Worth's economic future. The letter had been passed on to the press by an irate neighbor of a former Armour worker. A press conference was called in which the general objectives of the committee were emphasized, and the limited role of geographic mobility in the over-all program was explained.

To be sure, the long-standing and largely irrational rivalry between the two cities made for exceptional animosity. However, most communities resent seeing their population depleted, especially as past of a conscious program. Nonetheless, geographic mobility can be an avenue of adjustment, and should be used to whatever extent individuals can be encouraged to do so—although it should be recognized that community groups, including the local employment service office, may have great difficulty in publicizing anything containing the tacit admission that there is relatively less economic opportunity in the home town than other places.

Another major setback to the Fort Worth program was the inactivity of federal and state officials charged with the administration of MDTA. The federal training act had been passed shortly after the impending shutdown had been announced, and the committee was hopeful that programs could be quickly established in Fort Worth. Initial contacts were made at both federal and state levels. Congress had not yet appropriated funds for the program, but was expected to do so at any moment. The committee was told that programs for Fort Worth could be planned so that action could begin as soon as funds became available. Although MDTA programs in other parts of the country did start quickly, this expectation was not fulfilled in Texas. In any event, the standards for entrance to the early MDTA program were such that most of the former Armour workers probably would have been excluded. The net result of the committee's entreaties and complaints was virtually nil. No special help was received from the federal government in the Fort Worth retraining and placement effort. Ultimately, one former Armour worker coming within the committee's program entered an MDTA training course.

## Sioux City

The extent of community involvement was greatest in Sioux City. The committee representatives came into town in Oklahoma City and Fort Worth virtually unnoticed, but in Sioux City they were met at the airport by a delegation of civic leaders representing various aspects of community life. A Citizens' Re-employment Committee, composed of businessmen and public officials, had been established through local initiative shortly after the announcement of the closedown. The employment service had moved energetically into the situation, and had laid the groundwork for a special project to aid the workers facing displacement. Extensive interviewing and testing took place before the shutdown. In addition, state and federal officials had been alerted to the situation and were planning for coordinated measures. In this relatively small community, efforts to deal with the problems of displacement were a focus of attention and the object of concern by officials at all levels.

A rapid succession of steps was taken to give content to the community program. The necessary forms to establish MDTA courses were filed in Des Moines. The Citizens Re-employment Committee helped canvass the labor market for job opportunities. The employment service made the placement program a reality to the individuals seeking employment. Widespread press, radio, and TV coverage helped to foster a sympathetic attitude in the community.

Nevertheless, even this vigorous community response misfired at several important points. The public school system in Sioux City was seriously deficient in resources for adult vocational courses geared to employment as distinct from avocational interests. The few private schools in the area covered a limited range of subjects and therefore did not provide sufficient supplementary facilities for a successful retraining program. It was clear that an important preliminary step was the augmentation of existing vocational educational resources, and that MDTA could play a critical role in this area. Here the cooperation of the local school board was essential. Their cooperation was never forthcoming, and efforts to win their support led at last to political and ideological controversy.

The chief issue was the request for the school board's approval of the use of its premises for two MDTA-sponsored courses, one in auto mechanics and the other in auto body and fender repair. The existing school facilities were usable for the mechanics course if supplemented with modern equipment; the body and fender course required a complete new installation. Both additions were to be financed from MDTA funds, and under MDTA regulations it was necessary to offer the local school board first opportunity to administer the program. If the school board refused, administrative responsibility could be assumed by state or federal agencies—an alternative that was clearly undesirable. The problems of administering the courses from Des Moines or from Washington were formidable, and prolonged delays were certain to ensue. In addition, it was important to involve the school board so that it could assume the administrative responsibility for other MDTA courses that might be established in the immediate future.

The invitation to the school board for assuming the responsibility was first rejected, then reconsidered, and then rejected once again. Following the intervention of the Citizens Re-employment Committee, a second reconsideration took place. The final decision permitted the use of school facilities for the auto mechanics course, but stipulated that the school board was not to administer the course or to allow the expansion of its facilities to accommodate the course in auto body and fender repair. Consequently, subsequent MDTA programs would have to be assumed by agencies outside of Sioux City.

What factors led the school board to reject what appeared to be a wholly constructive activity initiated in the interests of the community and supported by the mayor, the city manager, and a group of respected citizens? The initial rejection was apparently based on a dislike of having the federal government intrude upon the Sioux City educational system, along with a fear that hidden costs would be imposed even though all costs were completely reimbursable under the MDTA program. A further complication was that if the school system accepted responsibility for MDTA programs, the salary of the director of vocational education would be supplemented to a degree that he would be earning more than the school superintendent to whom he was responsible.

When the matter was first reconsidered, two additional factors came into play. At a special meeting, representatives of the U.S.

Bureau of Employment Security indicated that they or the state had the right—and the obligation—to administer the retraining programs in Sioux City if the school board refused the opportunity. This was interpreted as an implied threat, and served to confirm the suspicions of local people that MDTA could be the vehicle for federal intervention, and perhaps for "domination" of the community's schools. In addition, some garage and auto repair shop owners had come to the school board with doubts of the validity of the labor market survey made by the employment service that showed a need for more manpower in their field.

Before a second reconsideration of the program, representatives of the Automation Fund Committee, working with the Citizens Re-employment Committee and the employment service, made a concerted effort to build support for the proposal and to offer a persuasive case. At a critical open hearing held by the school board and attended by some fifty people, including the head of the local Chamber of Commerce, arguments were presented by a variety of local and state people. A letter endorsing the proposal was sent to the board by the chairman of the Citizens Re-employment Committee, and the city council was enlisted in support of the proposal. A week after the meeting, the school board's final decision on the issue was made.

The *Des Moines Register*, a newspaper that is widely read and highly influential in Sioux City, commented editorially under the heading, "Sioux City Says No!":

The Board's decision should be examined against Sioux City's employment situation. Closing of the Armour plant has given the city one of the highest unemployment rates in the state. More than half of the 1,100 workers Armour laid off three months ago still are listed as unemployed. . . . Approximately 250 former Armour workers, including 170 of those now out of work, have expressed an interest in the retraining . . . A federal training program apparently will proceed in Sioux City, with or without the school board. State vocational education officials have said they will operate the program themselves and, if they fail, will ask federal agencies to take charge. Turning the training over to the state, however, means further delay. Leaving the program to the state also guarantees exactly what the Sioux City school board feared most: control by outside agencies. . . . If the school board had chosen to remain in the program, local authorities would have prepared the curricula, hired the instructors, arranged for facilities and supervised the classes. But, now, control of all this will pass to state and federal agencies. At the same time, Sioux City stands to lose the psychological advantage of being able to run its own program and solve its own unemployment problems. The president of the Sioux City Chamber of Commerce (speaking as a private citizen) recognized this when he advised board members that industrialists interested in new plant locations would look more favorably on the city if local agencies were administering the training program. . . . Unless someone acts soon to provide new skills and job opportunities for these workers, Sioux City may lose many of them as potential trainees and as citizens.

A year after the shutdown, ninety-three individuals were enrolled in MDTA programs, although four had been forced to go to other cities to do so. Nevertheless, the prophecy of delay by the *Des Moines Register* was fully realized. Once the initiative and responsibility for administering the retraining program were shifted from the local community, it became enmeshed in a network of red tape which tied together the various vocational educational agencies at the state and local levels. Ultimately, a state coordinator was appointed for the Sioux City project. But his effectiveness was sharply impaired by a lack of familiarity with local conditions and by the necessity—or proclivity—for checking with Des Moines before concrete action was taken. As a matter of fact, the automobile body and fender repair course—the *cause célèbre* of the Sioux City project—did not get under way until October of 1964, even though the funds had been allocated for the program in June, 1963. Requests made by the local office of the employment service for four other courses languished for nearly a year. The one triumph was a course in retail meatcutting, for which facilities were found by the manager of the local employment service office in cooperation with the Automation Fund

Committee. As a whole, the Sioux City experience revealed that community involvement in the problems of displaced workers did not automatically ensure the success of the program. In fact, it could cut deeply in either direction.

## A Note on Kansas City

Although the Kansas City project was still in its formative stage in early 1965, brief reference may be made to the involvement of the community there. The committee took an approach somewhere between that in Fort Worth and that in Sioux City. Because the number of Armour workers involved was relatively small in proportion to the Kansas City labor market as a whole, no attempt was made to involve representative elements of the community, as in Sioux City. The committee shied away from any equivalent of the Citizens Re-employment Committee, for fear of unduly complicating the initiation and administration of its program. Further difficulties could be expected because two large communities were encompassed by the metropolitan labor market. The Committee did, however, arrange a meeting of representatives of such community groups such as the Chamber of Commerce, the public school administration, and the city government to outline its goal and plan of operation. The general objective of the committee was to elicit the cooperation of these agencies without setting up a new group to yoke them together in the decision-making process.

On the other hand, the committee worked closely from the beginning with the local public employment services, which were to assume the heaviest responsibility for placement and for the retraining of the displaced workers under the auspices of MDTA. Meetings were held with the top administrators of the Bureau of Employment Security in Washington to discuss the situation and to plan for action in Kansas City. This meeting was quickly followed up by planning sessions at the local level. Thereafter, committee representatives and employment service officials worked closely together on specific elements of the program. The task of working with government agencies was simplified because the regional officers of the Bureau of Employment Security and the Department of Health, Education and Welfare were located in Kansas City, so that lengthy communications were not necessary to obtain approval for particular measures. Thus in Kansas City, the committee engaged in intensive collaboration with *specialized agencies*, but made no attempt to enlist the community at large. At the outset of the program, at least, this approach appeared well suited to the Kansas City situation.

## Public Actions and the Adjustment Process

The experiences of the committee provide some basis for general comment concerning the role of community action and government procedures in the adjustment to large-scale labor displacement, and may help in considering other possible forms of cooperation between public and private groups in such ventures.

1. Formal community involvement is inevitable, and largely desirable, when a major displacement occurs in a relatively small city. In larger cities, however, where specialized agencies are available for coping with the problems at hand, involving the total community is not necessary and indeed may be cumbersome.

Involving the community means bringing the groups concerned into the picture at an early state, while planning and policy formulation are under way, if those groups are to make an enduring commitment to the program. If community groups form at a later stage, they may do so in reaction against what are viewed as undesirable aspects of the program. Community groups can be helpful in a variety of ways. They can cultivate a sympathetic atmosphere in which to carry through particular measures. They can help to provide a pool of general information about the community and its resources, and in gaining access to local business leaders. They can help in collecting job leads. And they may use their influence to remove barriers to action at critical points in the program.

Deep involvement with the formal structure of the community is not an unmixed blessing, however. Local groups can exercise negative as well as positive power, and the problem can become acute if they use that power to block essentially administrative processes. Local politics and prejudices can also intrude excessively, particularly when the aims of the private group are at variance with customary attitudes, as toward racial discrimination in Fort Worth. Under any circumstances, a private group such as the Automation Fund Committee must maintain its independence and freedom of action. Inevitably, when a clash of values occurs, those prevalent in the community will have an impact on the private program; but with reasonable sensitivity to the local situation, independent private agencies may still hope to modify it.

Whether the city is small or large, efforts to deal with major displacement problems will necessarily impinge on the wider community. The critical questions are the extent of formal collaboration with community groups and the tactics to be employed when a challenge to community attitudes is required.

2. The public employment service is potentially the most valuable single community resource for working with displacement problems, regardless of the limitations under which it may sometimes operate. The contrasting experiences in Forth Worth and Sioux City suggest that vigorous efforts by the employment service, organized on a special project basis, can achieve better results than an independent placement program launched by a private group.

Giving the dominant role to the employment service does not mean that a private agency has no important functions. There are many ways in which a private group can be a welcome supplement to the activities of a vigorous Employment Service. In retrospect, it would appear that the independent placement activities of the committee in Fort Worth may have diminished the willingness of the local office to extend itself on behalf of the displaced workers by leading to an impression that the committee was a competitor. It is more effective to secure the deep involvement of the employment service from the beginning, so that it is committed to the success of the program. On the other hand, if the local employment service is lethargic or inept, or if it is not accepted by employers and workers, a private agency may be forced to work largely on its own. Even then, however, it must be remembered that the private agency can only be temporary, whereas the employment service is a permanent part of the community scene. In the long run, efforts to improve the performance and acceptability of the employment service may have a greater payoff for displaced workers than energetic solo ventures which are inevitably temporary.

3. Any effort on behalf of a particular group, no matter how gravely disadvantaged, fundamentally amounts to a request for special treatment in relation to other groups or individuals in the community. Accordingly, some justification must be offered for devoting general resources to the problems of a particular group. One argument for special treatment is founded on the notion of "economies of scale" in dealing with an essentially homogeneous group of individuals. Since these individuals do have a minimum common claim on general resources, a special program may actually reduce the aggregate expenditures on their behalf. A more convincing case can be presented if the request for a custom-made program is linked to a pledge of supplementary private support; and to this extent the Automation Fund Committee has been in a strong position, since it has been ready to commit substantial money and energy to an activity that benefits the entire community as well as the displaced workers. By such arguments the resistance to the "special treatment" approach may be minimized.

4. Programs calling for geographic mobility raise delicate problems for any agency based in the local community, and can usually be carried out with more discretion by a private group, thanks to its greater independence in the face of possible public reactions. In Sioux City, it will be recalled, a large number of people were transferred to other Armour plants and thus removed from the community. Because these transfers were part of a more general effort to aid those who remained in the community, no outspoken criticism was incurred. The Fort Worth–Dallas rivalry

is unique in many respects; nevertheless, the sensitivity exhibited in Fort Worth to any inference that economic prospects were less favorable there than in Dallas suggests the nature of the problem. Even in Sioux City, community groups preferred to have the initiative for the relocation of trainees come from the Automation Fund Committee.

5. The federal MDTA program is relatively new and obviously constitutes an important tool for dealing with labor displacement. That part of the program falling within the jurisdiction of the U.S. Department of Labor and the local employment service, insofar as Sioux City is at all representative, is administered with enthusiasm and skill. The energy has often been dissipated, however, in elaborate bureaucratic procedures imposed by those responsible for the educational aspects of the program. In addition, the parallel jurisdiction and administration by two government agencies can bring enormous frustration and delay at each stage of implementation. There is a pressing need for improved interdepartmental coordination and for better work among the various levels of government involved. The special project concept, giving a particular individual responsibility and reasonable discretion in handling the over-all program, may ameliorate the situation. Alternatively, the federal government may find it expeditious to contract with private groups, subject to carefully drawn conditions on the expenditure of public funds, but with responsibility and the authority to act lodged in one central place at the scene of the problem.

6. A remarkable change has occurred within the last decade in attitudes toward the problems of unemployment and large-scale displacement. Private and public concern have been accompanied by the marshaling of new resources. In both sectors there is a general willingness to experiment with new techniques. The fact is that communities no longer must go it alone in dealing with large-scale displacement. The challenge now is how to organize the public and private resources available into a comprehensive pattern of action so as to obtain maximum effectiveness.

# 8

*Primer for Policy: Some*

*Further Steps*

THE path traveled by the Automation Fund Committee has been marked by disappointment and by some modest achievements. At each major step, the committee has sought to revaluate its assumptions and the pragmatic techniques used to translate these assumptions into action. Both the failures and the successes have provided useful insights into the process of adjustment to large-scale labor displacement.

Some evidence that this learning process has been constructive is afforded simply by noting the number of people who were aided in any way by the committee in each successive case. In Oklahoma City, the committee's efforts had a direct significance for 58 individuals, or 14 per cent of the displaced workers. At the time the Fort Worth project was terminated, 359 individuals, counting those in training programs, or 36 per cent of the plant labor force, had been helped as a result of retraining and placement in the labor market or with other Armour units.

In Sioux City over 600 persons, more than 50 per cent of those affected by the plant shutdown, came within the scope of the programs established by the committee alone and in conjunction with government agencies, and over 200 more participated in the interplant transfer plan. Although the Kansas City project was still unfolding in early 1965, at least 400 workers had already benefited from the various adjustment measures.

These quantitative gains clearly reflect some qualitative improvement as well. Successive placement efforts have been carried with more urgency and on a more comprehensive basis. The training programs have been more ambitious and of longer duration, with more generous financial support for the trainee during his course of study. And the transfer program has operated with a notable measure of success. Government units have entered the picture with increasing vigor and on a wider scale, reflecting both new legislation and some improvements in administration. In addition, many displaced workers have benefited from severance or retirement pay, while those selecting the interplant option received Technological Adjustment Pay during the period of unemployment between shutdown and assignment to another plant, and moving allowances when the transfer was actually consummated.

When a comparison is made with the earlier shutdowns, in which relatively limited efforts were made to ease the transition for displaced workers, it is clear that there has been significant progress. On the other hand, it is equally evident that those reemployed outside Armour do not enjoy the same economic well-being as in their former jobs. For the typical worker displaced after long attachment to a particular plant and industry, the process of adjustment will usually be an arduous one. Modest achievement, then, is no justification for complacency. Instead, it offers an empirical basis for continued efforts, and a stimulus to further experiment with whatever appropriate techniques may be at hand. On this basis, certain observations may be offered as guides to public and private programs for active labor market administration.

## Lessons for Labor Market Administration

1. The success of any program for the transfer, retraining, and placement of workers affected by permanent displacement, no matter how well financed or how energetically administered, is closely dependent upon the state of the labor market. When unemployment is high or rising, the jobs are simply not available to absorb the displaced workers. The experiences in Oklahoma City, Sioux City, and Fort Worth reemphasized this truism.

Efforts toward the immediate placement of retrained workers were significantly more successful in Fort Worth than in Oklahoma City. Prospects for the Oklahoma City retrainees improved only when local employment rebounded from a sharp downturn. In Sioux City the limited scope of the labor market led to emphasis on the interplant transfer option and an active consideration of job opportunities in other communities, in connection with a program of retraining and placement.

In this way, conditions in the labor market will have a fundamental influence on the design of the program and on the choices by individual workers among the various options open to them. Even after allowance is made for the improvements in the administration of the interplant transfer plan, the workers' more favorable response to the plan in Sioux City than in Fort Worth can be explained, in part, by the differences in the state of the labor market.

In recent debates, economists have been divided over whether current unemployment should be blamed on structural factors or on a lack of aggregate demand. The Armour experiences provide some support to both sides. They reveal that a high level of aggregate demand is essential to the success of the various labor market policies advocated by those who emphasize structural problems. Programs that involve retraining and placement go hand in hand with fiscal measures, such as the reduction in tax rates, designed to stimulate effective demand.

2. Regardless of the particular labor market framework, advance notice of major employee displacement to the workers, the union, and the appropriate government and community agencies is a procedural prerequisite for constructive action. It gives the various organizations some time to organize their programs, and permits individuals to adjust their own plans, as well as to consider the various available options with care. The 90-day notice of the plant closings in Fort Worth, Sioux City, and Kansas City, as contrasted to the abrupt shutdown in Oklahoma City, made an important difference in the scope and quality of subsequent pro-

grams. Moreover, contrary to a widespread notion, the employees' productivity typically has not fallen in the period between the announcement and the final closing.

Although a 90-day notice serves many useful purposes, some of the actions taken within this framework in response to major labor displacement have still amounted to a "crash" program. A notification period tends to go through three stages: an initial period of absorbing the shock of the announcement, during which little constructive thought can be expected; a period of planning for the development of options and the administrative arrangements for making them operative; and finally, a period of choice and action, during which individuals examine the alternatives and arrive at an orderly decision.

It is therefore apparent that if it is or can be made economically and technically feasible, there should be at least six months', and preferably a year's advance notice. Where the notice is short or nonexistent, those involved have little opportunity to formulate or implement plans to remedy the situation. Further, if the stages of planning and choice fall into the period following the shutdown, some possibilities may abort—as in the Oklahoma City transfer proposal—and many individuals may drift away without ever learning the options open to them.

The problems of a "crash" program are particularly evident when the education level of the employees is low, so that effective retraining for many types of jobs is difficult to achieve. Wherever workers, sensing an impending shutdown, improved their skills through an extensive period of training, they were in a far better position to adapt than most of their fellows. For the greater part, however, workers with limited education had insufficient time to remedy these deficiencies and were often foreclosed from attractive retraining opportunities. The new MDTA provisions underwriting literacy training hold some promise in this area. Nonetheless, it is probable that displaced workers with heavy financial obligations will be reluctant to participate. A prolonged period of advance notice would give the worker facing displacement the chance to build up his basic educational background in preparation for the adjustment process. Alternatively and preferably, however, basic education should receive far more attention during times of normal employment than it now does. Workers themselves, as well as their unions and managements, could do far more under such circumstances than during even a prolonged preshutdown period.

3. When a fall in employment is foreseen for an individual establishment, preventive measures can be taken even though the exact magnitude and incidence of the displacement cannot be predicted at the time. Management can and typically does follow a policy of minimizing displacement by not hiring and allowing normal turnover to bring about a reduction in the work force. This normal economic process provides the means by which many kinds of adjustment can be made; but in a plant shutdown the limitations of a narrow approach to attrition are obvious. For a multiplant company, anything so complete and abrupt as a plant shutdown means that the attrition concept can be a useful instrument of policy only as part of an interplant transfer plan.

The interplant transfer plan developed by the two meatpacking unions and Armour and Company attempted to build such a broad attrition base while minimizing interplant tensions among the workers. It will be recalled that the plan established a cutoff date after which newly hired workers in any Armour meatpacking plant covered by the bargaining agreement were subject to bumping by senior employees whom the shutdown of another plant had displaced. In effect, this company-wide approach amounted to a "stockpiling" of attrition against future contingencies. As contrasted with a plan that permits transferees to bump on the basis of full seniority, the Armour system had a limited immediate potential for mitigating the consequences of plant shutdowns. However, it has grown in importance with the passage of time, subject to the limitation that aggregate displacement does not exceed the number of employees with seniority subsequent to the start of the plant.

The linking of company-wide attrition to the implementation of the transfer program has had a more subtle and fundamental influence on the committee's operational perspective. That is, in order to exploit effectively the potentialities of the plans it has been necessary to engage in at least a rough form of long-term manpower planning. Any program for the redistribution of economic opportunities must be founded on a knowledge of the employment base that will exist over the time allowed for the adjustment process. An appreciation of these relationships has induced the parties to take some tentative steps to assess manpower requirements over a period of time that extends beyond the date of the next plant shutdown.

4. The possibility of transfer does not, of course, mean that this option will always be exercised. To be sure, there is considerable evidence that many workers are reluctant to change their place of residence even when they have an opportunity to transfer to a plant of the same company, covered by the same collective bargaining contract. The experiences in Sioux City and Kansas City reveal, however, that transfer and relocation can be an attractive alternative where the circumstances are in large measure subject to the parties' control. Here, it will be remembered, a concerted effort was made to place the transfer option clearly before the work force. In addition, one small but significant change was made in the transferees' rights. Each individual was allowed a trial period in the new location, giving him an option to return within six months without sacrificing his severance pay. Thus the risks of experimenting with a transfer were sharply diminished. The transfer option was also made more attractive when, as in the Kansas City–Worthington case, the committee made strenuous efforts to promote a favorable reception in the receiving community. Similarly, the degree to which other elements of uncertainty are removed strongly influences the decision to transfer. In this respect, the Sioux City study revealed that job security at the new location and the physical conditions of the new job were decisive factors to many employees contemplating transfer.

That transfer plans must be adapted to the needs of the potential transferees warrants emphasis, especially since the initial experiences in Armour and other companies may lead, and have led, to unduly pessimistic conclusions concerning geographical relocation as a method for dealing with large-scale displacement. Relocation usually involves a difficult adjustment for the worker and his family, but many will take this step under propitious conditions. Continued experiment with relocation is necessary in order to adapt this policy to a wide range of circumstances.

The dislocations caused by plant shutdowns are usually so severe that it is not enough to focus on opportunities within the bargaining relationship. Hence, any program must transcend these corporate boundaries, providing alternatives and support for the displaced workers.

5. For those who left the confines of the firm, severance pay provided a financial cushion against the economic shock of displacement. In general, severance pay appears to have played a constructive role in the adjustment process. It does not appear that the prospect of receiving a sizable lump sum, by itself, has exercised an undue influence on the employees' selection of a particular displacement option. Similarly, most of the recipients of severance pay seem to have used these funds prudently during the adjustment period, and to have resisted the temptation of extravagant consumption.

The problems that have arisen in connection with this program have largely been outside the control of the workers themselves. In the first place, a large proportion of the separation allowance has often gone to pay debts, leaving little or nothing over. As a policy issue, there are no obvious solutions to this problem. However, since one of the major claimants of the severance allowance is frequently the company credit union, some provision should be made in the organization's bylaws to permit extended repayment of loans in the event that a member-debtor is permanently displaced from the firm. Since the credit union is controlled by its members, such a change is at least within the realm of possibility.

In the second place, a few states have denied unemployment compensation to the recipients of separation pay until they have technically "exhausted" the latter. It is hardly consistent with enlightened policy for public authorities to deflate the "financial cushion" that has been created by private means to deal with unemployment. Certainly, the modification of these administrative rulings is in order so that private and public programs are complementary rather than conflicting.

By contrast with separation pay, the administration of private and public programs for retirement income have been so closely integrated that withdrawal from the labor market can be a real option for the older displaced worker. The amendment of the Social Security Act to permit receiving benefits at age 62 is an important element in the special retirement program negotiated by Armour and Company and the two meatpacking unions. Under this arrangement, displaced workers who are 55 years of age and who have at least twenty years of service, can receive a special "1½" pension until they are 62, when they are eligible for OASI. By reducing the direct cost of early retirement, the change in the public program helped pave the way for a supporting private program. Moreover, the response of the eligible Armour workers indicates that this option can be an attractive one to the older employee who otherwise must find his way in the labor market.

6. The cumulative experience of the committee with various placement efforts suggests that the most useful role a private group can play in facilitating the re-employment of displaced workers is to supplement the activities of public agencies and to concentrate on cases that involve unique problems of individual adjustment. It is extremely difficult for private groups such as the Automation Fund Committee to mount a broadly effective placement campaign. The employment service has existing facilities and an operative organization, it is a permanent part of the community, and it has an interstate network of communications through which it can develop a broadly based placement effort. In

this area, private efforts can complement those of a public agency; however, the role of the public agency should be paramount.

The usefulness of the federal-state employment service is greatly enhanced where its activities are organized and implemented on a "special project" basis. This approach has the advantage of mobilizing administrative personnel who have special skills and knowledge and, perhaps more importantly, of energizing and raising the aims of the people in the local office. The Sioux City and Kansas City projects, where the employment service dealt vigorously and systematically with mass displacement, gave credence to the theoretical benefits of the "special project" concept. By contrast, the programs carried out in Oklahoma City and Fort Worth indicate that the use of routine procedures to handle mass layoff problems is not likely to produce satisfactory results.

7. No matter how well conceived a placement campaign may be, formidable handicaps may be imposed by the fact that many displaced workers, who have been long accustomed to a specific job, have no particular skill to offer a prospective employer in another industry. If these workers are not to be relegated to the unskilled labor pool, some form of retraining and skill development must be brought into play. Records compiled by the Automation Fund Committee, particularly in Fort Worth, demonstrate that workers with limited educational backgrounds can profit from retraining for occupations in demand in the labor market. A successful program, however, must set up criteria for allocating retraining opportunities to individuals, for the facilities used, for the financial support of the program and the trainees, and for the general administrative energy with which the program is to be carried out.

To decide whether a potential trainee will be able to meet the demands of a specific course, a broad evaluation is necessary. This evaluation should include such factors as education, test scores, prior experience, attitudes, and motivation. Any program that aims to help the unemployed will be self-defeating if it imposes criteria that exclude those who need help most. At the outset of the MDTA program the employment service appeared excessively stringent in qualifying people for training opportunities. In Fort Worth, only one out of 170 Armour retrainees was enrolled in a MDTA course; the rest drew on the support provided by the Automation Fund Committee. The meager coverage of the government program reflected, in part, the delay in establishing MDTA courses in Texas. Few former Armour employees would have been accepted in any event, however, because of the rigid application of the General Aptitude Test Battery scores. The GATB is a useful tool in helping to determine the general aptitudes of potential retrainees. But it is foolhardy, and frequently inequitable, to disqualify applicants for particular courses because they were a few points below the specified minimum in a single trait—especially when the applicants have not been in a formal testing situation for as long as twenty years.

The matter of applicants' test scores may superficially appear minor. Nonetheless, it is through just such minutiae that opportunities for self-improvement may be foreclosed to the hard core of unemployed, and the effectiveness of the Manpower Act and parallel private efforts blunted accordingly. Employment service counselors often have a rich background in evaluating the capabilities of workers, and should be allowed to broaden their evaluations to include every possible factor. This approach was taken in the Sioux City project, and a much larger number of displaced Armour workers enjoyed the benefits of MDTA than could otherwise have done so. No major problems of quality or performance were reported to have arisen among the retrainees.

8. The importance of adequate training facilities to the success of any retraining program cannot be overemphasized. Bad training is usually worse than no training at all. Poorly equipped private schools seeking quick returns at the expense of displaced workers do damage to the workers and to the basic concept of effective retraining. In Fort Worth, the public training facilities available to whites were outstanding. Since these were not open to Negroes,

however, in order to serve them the committee was forced to resort to private schools where the quality of instruction was highly variable.

In Sioux City, the major problem was the general inadequacy of facilities, a deficiency that greatly retarded the program. Some people were forced to go to distant cities for training. For others, courses were scheduled between 10 P.M. and 4 A.M. in order to have access to the limited facilities available. It is painfully evident from the Sioux City case that the hardship inevitable to any community that falls behind in providing educational resources will be all the greater when a crisis arises such as that precipitated by a major plant shutdown.

9. Occupational retraining programs must also provide adequate support and incentives for potential retrainees. Public attitudes toward providing compensation for retrainees often reflect the misguided notion that training is "loafing" and may degenerate into malingering. Effective training generally imposes a considerable hardship on the older, unemployed worker who is not accustomed to an intensive educational situation. Too limited financial support for those in training will be self-defeating, since retrainees, particularly those with extensive family responsibilities, will be forced to drop out of training before it is completed, in effect wasting the months already invested in this effort. Moreover, the legislation in Oklahoma, Texas, and Iowa that denied unemployment compensation benefits to workers who were enrolled in privately financed retraining courses, hampered the committee's program and put an onerous and unwarranted burden on the trainees. Considerable attention has been focused on this issue in recent years, and several states have taken appropriate corrective action.

10. The selection of trainees presumes their rapid enrollment in the designated retraining programs. This may sound like a truism, but in practice it can mean a prolonged and exasperating wait. In Sioux City, the advantages derived from systematic advance planning were largely nullified by the confusion and delays resulting from a

lack of coordination among the various government agencies involved. Up to sixteen months elapsed between the initial certification by the local employment service office of the need for a course in a particular occupation to the actual inception of the program.

These delays were largely attributable to the cumbersome bureaucratic machinery imposed by the Department of Health, Education and Welfare, and to a lack of a sense of urgency on the part of individual administrators. Sioux City as a community must share in the blame for the difficulties and delays in the MDTA program, since the school board's refusal of full cooperation with the program complicated immeasurably the problem of obtaining proper facilities. Every community has vital resources to contribute toward aiding displaced workers, and in making this contribution will serve its own interest as well. One of the important lessons of the Sioux City case is the need to tap community resources without subjecting the program to complications of procedure which make action ponderous or impossible. At the same time, involvement of community leaders at an early stage in the development of the program is an inevitable ingredient in a program conducted in any medium or small-sized city.

Failure to give rapid implementation to plans for vocational training may have serious consequences. To paraphrase a legal maxim, retraining delayed may be retraining denied. Too often, the displaced worker awaiting training will find some menial temporary position and will be reluctant to give up the job for training from which he can benefit only in the long run. His desire to hold on to the "bird in the hand" is often intensified by the depletion of his financial resources during the period of waiting. In other instances, the displaced workers will become discouraged by the lack of opportunities and may lapse into apathy or chronic economic dependence.

Recognition of the effect of delay upon the unemployed workers' willingness and ability to participate in a retraining program can be a dilemma for a private group. It can counsel a "client" to await the government program, all the while knowing that by the time it finally gets under way he may have become disenchanted with this option. Or, the private group may move ahead on its own initiative and more limited resources with the realization that the quality of the training obtained by sheer improvisation or by resort to private schools of dubious reputation may be inferior. Where these approaches were followed—in Sioux City and Fort Worth—the over-all effectiveness of the program was impaired. The early experience in Kansas City indicates that such a choice between two undesirable options may be unnecessary.

11. Even though the actual commencement of retraining may be an occasion for relief, if not self-congratulation, it is clear that the administration of programs for aiding displaced workers cannot be a "one-shot" affair. Such programs must be closely supervised over a long period of time. Once workers are enrolled in training courses, consideration must be given to their morale and progress. After completion of training, an effort may have to be made to get the person to seek and accept a job in the occupation for which he was trained. Several workers, for various reasons, were reluctant to move from a current job unrelated to the training to one that would more fully utilize newly acquired skills. Even when placement in training-related occupations is achieved, continued counseling should be available to guard against loss of confidence. Where layoffs occur, additional placement activities will be necessary. During the post-training period, workers may also be encouraged to augment their skills through further education. Thus, effective training and placement programs must follow the worker's re-entry into the labor market through a sequence of steps. These needs underscore the importance of building the employment service and its resources deeply into the structure of any program, even one that owes its inspiration to a private organization. The employment service will remain on the scene and can provide the long-term effort needed.

12. An important general objective of any program for dealing with employee displacement should be to cultivate a "sense of mobil-

ity" among the displaced. As revealed by these experiences, one of the formidable obstacles to effective readjustments to displacement is the lack of awareness on the part of the worker of alternative opportunities and of how to capitalize upon them. In most cases, the displaced worker will have been out of the labor market for a long period of time and will thus be ill prepared for the new challenge that is thrust upon him. In effect, the general objective of any remedial program is to re-equip the displaced worker for effective participation in the labor market. This process calls for a variety of tools—intensive counseling, instruction in the techniques of job-seeking, information concerning possible employment opportunities over a wide market, and a knowledge of prevailing wage levels and occupational training. Essentially, governmental and private programs can only help the jobless to help themselves; but this aim cannot be achieved unless the worker has a "sense of mobility" in the labor market.

13. The varied experiences of the committee substantiate the view that there is no single and simple approach to the problems of worker displacement. Different groups and individuals have sharply different needs. Recognition of and adaptation to these differences is a prerequisite to any successful attack on the problems of displacement. Some workers have marketable skills, and a good placement program will help them. Others can benefit from retraining. For still others, transfer to another plant, if at all possible, may be preferable. Retirement options may be available to those in the upper age categories. Essentially any remedial program must consist of a "package" of possible measures for helping particular individuals or groups. Behind it must be a careful and patient program for counseling individual workers about their options so that they can intelligently assess the advantages and pitfalls of the alternatives open to them. It is critically important to avoid overcommitment to any one means of attacking the problem of large-scale labor displacement, and to include in any remedial program as diverse and broad a package of policy tools as possible.

## A *Final Note*

There has been much discussion in this country of displacement and unemployment as problems of broad national significance. In response to this stimulus, public programs have been evolved that potentially may aid large numbers of people. Some are well developed and others are still in the experimental stage. Private programs, too, have been established to satisfy special needs. Such efforts, including those of the Automation Fund Committee, have gone through a process of trial and error, of success and disappointment. There is much to be learned and much to be done. Further research is needed on the factors that influence worker mobility. Additional thought must be given to the optimal methods for carrying out and financing occupational retraining. Concerted measures must be taken to organize the channels of information in the labor market.

Yet already the major elements of active manpower policies are becoming visible. What will be decisive now is not the devising of "bold new ideas" or the commitment of large additional sums of money—even though substantial resources are clearly needed. What must be recognized is that big programs mean something only when they fit the needs of particular situations and are helpful to particular individuals. This is the task that challenges our talents for administration. The numbers involved in the projects described here are small as compared to the long-run national problem. Many of the measures that have been tried have not worked; others have been moderately successful. From these experiences, however, has emerged the general conviction that given adequate resources, the program most likely to succeed is the one that remains flexible enough to deal with the individual within the framework of his problems. This objective may be as difficult to achieve in dealing with labor displacement as in other areas of social and economic policy, but the attempt must be made.

*Contract Provisions Governing the*

*Operation of the Automation*

*Fund Committee*[1]

It is recognized that the meatpacking industry is undergoing significant changes in methods of production, processing, marketing, and distribution. Armour's modernization program is vital to its ability to compete and grow successfully, thus providing a reasonable return on capital invested in the enterprise and providing the assurance of continued employment for the employees under fair standards of wages, benefits, and working conditions. Jobs are directly dependent upon making Armour products desirable to present and future customers from the viewpoint of quality and price.

Mechanization and new methods to promote operating and distributing efficiencies affect the number of employees required and the manner in which they perform their work. Technological improvement may result in the need for developing new skills and the acquiring of new knowledge by the employees. In addition, problems are created for employees affected by these changes that require the joint consideration of the company and the unions.

The company and the unions have in this and in past agreements provided benefits to soften the effect of some of these changes where employees are laid off or terminated. However, it is recognized that these problems require continued study to promote employment opportunities for employees affected by the introduction of more efficient methods and technological changes.

The company, therefore, agrees with the unions to continue the

[1] As it appears in the 1961 Agreement in which six specific duties were added to those in the 1959 Agreement.

Automation Fund established on September 1, 1959. The Automation Fund shall continue to be administered by a committee of nine, composed of four representatives of management and two representatives selected by each of the two unions, and an impartial chairman selected by mutual agreement of the parties.

The management and the unions shall each pay for the expenses of their respective representatives on the committee.

The fees and expenses of the impartial chairman shall be paid by the fund.

The committee is also authorized to utilize the fund for the purpose of studying the problems resulting from the modernization program and making recommendations for their solution, promoting employment opportunities within the company for those employees affected, training qualified employees in the knowledge and skill required to perform new and changed jobs so that the present employees may be utilized for this purpose to the greatest extent possible, and providing allowances towards moving expenses for employees who transfer from one plant to another of the company's plants in accordance with the procedures provided in Article XXIII (Interplant Transfer Rights). It is agreed, however, that the fund shall not be used to increase present separation pay benefits or TAP benefits.

The committee should also continue to consider other programs and methods that might be employed to promote continued employment opportunities for those affected.

Except as explicitly provided otherwise below, the findings and recommendations of the committee shall not be binding upon the parties but shall be made to the company and to the unions for their further consideration.

In addition, the committee shall make determinations and formulate procedures under the terms of the master agreement as follows:

First . . . prescribe the form, formulate the procedures and determine the extent in which the company shall make seniority list information available to the unions.
Second . . . determine the number of calendar days within which an employee shall file a written request of transfer to another plant.
Third . . . define a proper offer of transfer and formulate rules and procedures providing for termination of an employee's right of transfer on refusal of such an offer of transfer.

Fourth . . . formulate rules for limiting the number of transfers into any bargaining unit in any one year.

Fifth . . . determine the allowance toward moving expense for employees who transfer in accordance with the procedures set forth in Article XXIII.

Sixth . . . define a replacement plant.

*Members of the Automation Fund*

*Committee and Others Who*

*Participated in Its Work*

1. Present membership of the committee is as follows:

*Co-Chairmen*

Clark Kerr
President, University of California

George P. Shultz
Dean, Graduate School of Business
University of Chicago

| *Union Representatives* | *Company Representatives* |
|---|---|
| Amalgamated Meat Cutters and Butcher Workmen of North America, AFL-CIO | Harold E. Brooks Vice President |
| Russell E. Dresser Vice President and Director Packinghouse Division | Walter E. Clark Vice President Labor Relations |
| James H. Wishart Research Director | Clifton B. Cox Vice President Foods Division |
| United Packinghouse Food & Allied Workers, AFL-CIO | Frederick R. Livingston Kaye, Scholer, Fierman, Hays & Handler |
| Ralph Helstein President | |
| Jesse Prosten Director of Contract Administration | |

2. The first executive director of the committee, serving in the formative period of 1959–61, was Robben W. Flemming, then professor of law, University of Illinois and now provost, University of Wisconsin. Others who have served as committee members are: for Armour, William J. Ohl, general manager, Food Engineering Division, and Fred C. Klasing, vice president, Foods Division; and for the UPWA, Howard McDermott, director, Wage Rate Department.

3. The committee's Oklahoma City project was directed by Edwin Young, dean of the College of Letters and Science, University of Wisconsin. Arnold R. Weber, professor at the Graduate School of Business, University of Chicago, and James Stern, professor at the University of Wisconsin, have served with the public members of the committee and have taken prime responsibility for various activities: Weber for the Fort Worth project and, with Eaton H. Conant, professor at the Graduate School of Business, University of Chicago, for the Sioux City project; and Stern, with Edward B. Jakubauskas, professor at Iowa State University, James Robinson, professor at the University of Missouri, and Owen A. Tapper, professor at the University of Wisconsin, for the Kansas City, Eau Claire, and Worthington projects. Full-time work for the committee was undertaken with great ability and dedication by the following women: Mrs. Jane Hostler in Oklahoma City, Mrs. Maxine Johnson in Fort Worth, Miss Gertrude Wolfe in Sioux City, and Mrs. Allie Jones in Kansas City.

4. Studies have been made for the committee by the following individuals: Norman M. Bradburn, professor at the Graduate School of Business and National Opinion Research Center, University of Chicago, on worker choices between transfer and severance after a plant shutdown; Milton Derber, professor at the Institute of Labor and Industrial Relations, University of Illinois, on the economics and employment prospects in the meatpacking industry; Bernt O. Larson, professor at the College of Engineering, University of Illinois, on maintenance skills for automated equipment; Joseph Pichler, research assistant, Graduate School of Business, University of Chicago, on employment experience of displaced workers in Sioux City, Iowa; S. Herbert Unterberger, Philadelphia, Pennsylvania, on the structure and uses of severance pay; Arnold R. Weber, professor at the Graduate School of Business, University of Chicago, on interplant transfer programs and on provisions for advance notice of plant closings; and

Richard C. Wilcock and Walter H. Franke, professors at the Institute of Labor and Industrial Relations, University of Illinois, on the employment experiences of workers displaced in Columbus, Ohio; Fargo, North Dakota; East St. Louis, Illinois; and Oklahoma City, Oklahoma.

*Publicly Available Materials*

*Resulting from the Work of the*

*Automation Fund Committee*

Automation Fund Committee. *Progress Report* (June, 1961).

Bradburn, Norman M. "Interplant Transfer: The Sioux City Experience," A Report to the Automation Fund Committee, Amalgamated Meat Cutters and Butcher Workmen of North America, United Packinghouse, Food and Allied Workers, and Armour and Company (Report #98, National Opinion Research Center, University of Chicago, 1964).

Conant, Eaton H. "Report on Transfer, Retraining, and Placement Experience of Workers Displaced by Shutdown of the Armour Plant in Sioux City, Iowa" (Automation Fund Committee, Mimeographed, 1965). A condensation of this report appeared in U.S. Department of Labor, *Monthly Labor Review*, November, 1965.

Shultz, George P., and Weber, Arnold R. "Report on Placement and Retraining Experience of Workers Displaced by Shutdown of the Armour Plant in Fort Worth, Texas" (Mimeographed, 1963).

Weber, Arnold R. "The Interplant Transfer of Displaced Employees," *Adjusting to Technological Change*, G. Somers *et al.*, editors (Harper & Row, 1963).

Weber, Arnold R., and Taylor, David P. "Procedures for Employee Displacement: Advance Notice of Plant Shutdown," *Journal of Business*, July, 1963.

Wilcock, Richard C., and Franke, Walter H. *Unwanted Workers* (The Free Press of Glencoe, 1963).

Young, Edwin. "The Armour Experience," *Adjusting to Technological Change*, G. Somers *et al.*, editors (Harper & Row, 1963).

*Recommendations for Public*

*Policy Made by the Committee*

*in 1961*

1. The events of recent years have made it clear that there is a vast change taking place in the nature of jobs. Unskilled and semiskilled labor often most readily lends itself to automation. Also there has been a noticeable shift from production to service industries, and from production to clerical or semiprofessional jobs. This means that the relatively unskilled and poorly educated employee finds himself at a severe disadvantage in the labor market. The jobs of the future will require better educated applicants. In this connection it is disquieting to read the prognostication of the United States Department of Labor that three out of ten of the 26,000,000 young people who will be seeking jobs during the 1960s will have dropped out of high school without receiving diplomas. Two and one-half million of them will not even have finished grade school. These facts lead us to the conclusion that the country's educational programs and their relationship to future employment must be studied by private as well as local and federal governmental agencies, and that early action must be taken.

2. Workers need much more help than they now get from the loosely coordinated state employment services. Every study which has been made, including our own, shows that public employment services play a minor role in finding jobs for individuals seeking work. Not all of this is the fault of the employment service. It may not require listing of vacancies, and by tradition the majority of employers do not hire through such services. Moreover, discrimination based on age and race may be beyond the control of the employment service. Nevertheless, it is hard to believe that a much more efficient

and effective organization cannot be developed. Workers know little or nothing about the kinds of jobs which are plentiful in other localities or are likely to be plentiful in their own locality in the days ahead. Neither workers nor their immediate employers, who might like to help in finding new jobs for workers who will be displaced, have any satisfactory means of knowing whether there are jobs available in other geographical areas. Where jobs are available at a distance it may be both necessary and desirable to provide a system of loans or grants which would be available to workers for the purpose of inducing them to move to new areas. We note with satisfaction that in response to the President's request Congress has made funds available for expanded employment services, and that the Secretary of Labor has called for a far more active and aggressive employment service. We believe, incidentally, that not only must the employment service be "primarily a placement office to match workers to jobs," but in doing so it must provide counseling which will direct workers toward the kinds of jobs which will be available in the years ahead.

3. Unemployment compensation policies need reconsideration. It may be that the displaced employee's best prospect of a new job is to be found upon completing some kind of retraining. If so, it would make sense to allow him to complete such a course without having to interrupt the training to take an available job lest he lose his unemployment compensation. Several states have recognized this fact and amended their laws accordingly. We believe that others would be well advised to follow suit. A more serious question relates to the duration of unemployment compensation benefits. Prior to 1959 most states offered a maximum of twenty-six weeks of benefits. The recession of 1958 brought federal action which extended such benefits for an additional thirteen weeks at the option of the states. Our studies of the problems faced by displaced employees lead us to the conclusion that a reasonable period, beyond which unemployment benefits should not apply, is yet to be determined. It is apparent that extended unemployment benefits are no substitute for jobs, and ought not to be accepted as such. But in the formulation of a satisfactory public policy we believe the length of the period in which unemployment benefits will be paid should be open to objective analysis.

We also believe that state unemployment compensation laws should be amended to permit unemployed workers to draw benefits without regard to the fact that they may have received, or are now receiving, severance pay benefits. To deny unemployment compensation during this period negates the very purpose of severance pay.

4. The interrelationship between public and private pension plans is in serious need of study. At the end of 1960 the SEC reported that total assets of all pension funds in the United States, both public and private, exceeded $105 billion. Total receipts of pension funds from all sources were $4.4 billion, $300 million over the 1959 and $900 million over 1958 receipts.

Labor mobility is inhibited because severance of the immediate employer-employee relationship dissolves the private pension bond. Manpower allocations which may be required in a national emergency become extraordinarily complicated when one tries to resolve the private pension equities which may be involved. Plant closings, accompanied by permanent displacement, inevitably sever the private pension relationship and give rise to union demands for costly vesting provisions. For these and other reasons, the committee believes a major study designed to determine the desirability and feasibility of integrating private and public pension systems should be undertaken.

A second pension problem which is worthy of consideration during the present period of high unemployment, relates to optional early retirement. The committee members do not favor compulsory early retirement; but optional early retirement at age 62, as is presently being proposed, may have certain advantages during a period of substantial unemployment. It will be relatively meaningless, however, unless it is coupled with the removal of the present unrealistic restrictions on the amount of earnings which a retired person is allowed to accept without impairing his pension rights. The committee members believe that both of these points should be considered.

5. There is a clear correlation between livestock inventories and man hours of work in the packing industry. The recent census of agriculture revealed that cattle numbers are somewhat smaller than Department of Agriculture estimates had assumed, that sheep numbers, while leveling off during the last two years, have been in a decline for some time, and that hog production has shown no discernible upward trend since 1956. The use of excess grain products to feed livestock, which would in turn take the form of edible meat products for both domestic and foreign consumption, could contribute to the solution of several problems.

The committee members have not attempted to explore the intricacies of this problem, but they believe it is worthy of joint study by private and public bodies and they are prepared to seek the cooperation of the government in analyzing the issues which are involved and in developing a program of action.

6. Minimum-wage laws, as such, are not very meaningful when applied to industries whose wage structures are marked by sharp differentials. Many democratic countries in the Western world have resolved this problem through the imposition of industry standards. Without attempting to prejudge the end result, the committee members believe that a study of this issue would contribute to the solution of a difficult problem.

7. Governmental regulatory measures, however wise at their inception, can become unduly onerous under changed circumstances. For example, an antitrust consent decree, entered against the meatpacking industry in the 1920s, is now deemed by both the United Packinghouse Workers and the company representatives on the committee to be unrealistic when applied to current conditions. The committee members believe that a study of such regulatory measures might result in action which would encourage the kind of growth and expansion in the industry which is desirable from every point of view.

# INDEX

215